METACOGNITIVE CLARITY

Think Rigorously. Advance Democracy.

Dr. Paul J. Bloomberg, Isaac Wells, and St. Claire Adriaan

Copyrighted Material
Metacognitive Clarity: Think Rigorously. Advance Democracy.

Copyright © 2026 by Dr. Paul J. Bloomberg, Isaac Wells, and St. Claire Adriaan. All Rights Reserved.
No part of this publication may be reproduced, stored in a retrieval system, or transmitted, in any form or by any means—electronic, mechanical, photocopy, recording, or otherwise—without prior written permission from the publisher, except for the inclusion of brief quotations in a review.

For more information about this title or to order other books and/or electronic media, contact the publisher:
Mimi and Todd Press
1090 North Palm Canyon Drive
Suite B
Palm Springs, CA 92262
www.mimitoddpress.com

ISBN: 978-1-950089-27-7 (paperback)
ISBN: 978-1-950089-28-4 (epub)

Printed in the United States of America
Program Director: Paul J. Bloomberg
Publishing Manager: Tony Francoeur
Executive Director of Publishing: Isaac Wells
Development Editor: Dan Alpert
Copy Editor: Terri Lee Paulsen
Layout: HMD Publishing
Illustrations: Alison Cox
Cover Design: Alison Cox
Indexer: Maria Sosnowski
Office Manager: Leah Tierney

Content

FOREWORD 6

PART I. VISION AND ARCHITECTURE

Introduction 15
    Metacognitive Clarity: A New Vision for Learning.................................... 15
    Reflect and Act.. 23

Chapter 1. The Architecture of Metacognitive Clarity............................25
    Learner Identity: The Cornerstone of Metacognitive Clarity 25
    The Core Elements of Metacognitive Clarity... 32
    The Architecture Is Collaborative 33
    The Architecture Is Emotional 35
    Toward Transformative Possibility 36

Chapter 2. The Hidden Engine of Learning 38
    The Metacognitive Cycle.. 38
    Making Sense of Knowledge Types Through Metacognition................... 42
    Metacognition Shapes Leaders, Learners, and Liberators 43
    Bringing It All Together: From Tasks to Transformation 46

Chapter 3. The Conditions That Liberate Thinking...............................48
    Psychological Safety: The Crucible of Courageous Thinking................... 48
    Identity Affirmation: The Power of Story 49
    Belonging: Why Community Is the Root of Great Thinking................... 50
    Teaching the Craft of Metacognition: From Skill to Agency 51
    Dismantling Hidden Barriers to Metacognitive Access 53
    From Better Thinking to Democratic Action.. 54

Chapter 4. Educating the Whole Learner: Integrating Heart, Mind, and Community 56
    The Transformative SEL Imperative 57
    Neuroscience Insights: Connecting Heart and Mind............................... 63

PART II. DESIGNING FOR PRACTICE

Chapter 5. Clarity of Purpose 69
- Justice-Centered Learning Goals: Beyond Standards 70
- Anchoring Learning in Community, Contribution, and Criticality 76
- Clarity as a Democratic Act 77

Chapter 6. Clarity of Process: Illuminating the Invisible Path 78
- The Art of Explicitly Teaching Learning-to-Learn 78
- Weaving Metacognition Into Every Moment 81
- Making the Invisible Visible 86
- Honoring the Journey 87

Chapter 7. Clarity of Ownership 91
- Student-Led Reflection, Co-Assessment, and Goal Setting 91
- Elevating Learner Voice in Shaping Success Criteria 94
- Cultivating Habits of Mind for Deeper Ownership 96
- Structures for Authentic, Democratic Learning Environments 99
- From Shared Ownership to Civic Empowerment 101

PART III. SYSTEMS AND LEADERSHIP FOR METACOGNITIVE CLARITY

Chapter 8. Cultivating a Culture of Metacognitive Clarity 103
- Collaborative Inquiry for Metacognitive Clarity 103
- Metacognitive Equity Walks 109
- Student-Led Instructional Rounds 115
- Student Governance Councils 118
- Youth Empowered Stewardship (YES) 120
- From Democratic Aspiration to Metacognitive Reality 121

Chapter 9. Elevating Educator Capacity: Professional Learning for Metacognitive Impact ... 123
- From Pockets of Excellence to Systems of Impact 123
- Why Standards-Based Professional Learning Matters 124
- Families as Co-Learners in Professional Learning 126
- What Are Impact Teams? 128
- Cultivating Democratic Agency 131

Chapter 10. Amplifying Metacognitive Clarity Through Family–School Partnerships 134
    School–Family Partnerships Begin With Trust and Mutual Respect 135
    Understanding the Dual Capacity-Building Framework 138
    Families as Natural Metacognitive Experts 139
    Advancing Metacognitive Clarity With Families 140
    Family Engagement as a Democratic Practice 145
    Overcoming Common Barriers 146
    Family Engagement as Collective Agency 149

Chapter 11. The Future of Learning Is Metacognitive 151
    Advance Agency-Driven Approaches 153
    Moving From Compliance to Empowerment 154
    Cultivate Democratically Empowered, Self-Directed Learners 156
    Position Metacognitive Clarity as an Ethical Imperative for Equity 158
    Be Part of the Metacognitive Transformation 161

From Dream to Possibility 164

An Invitation to Metacognitive Transformation 165

Glossary 167

References 170

Index 176

FOREWORD

by Jeneca Parker-Tongue

Clarity is not only a way of seeing, but a way of shining. Like the brilliance of bright color radiating around the luminous black silhouette of a child on this book's cover, clarity illuminates the wholeness of learning and being. It reveals strength, possibility, and presence—reminding us that brilliance lives within every learner, waiting to be reflected back. In this light, we are reminded of that simple and powerful truth.

Joy Harjo (2023), U.S. Poet Laureate, Muscogee (Creek) Nation member, and author of *Remember*—one of my children's favorite picture books—teaches: "Remember the earth whose skin you are: red earth, yellow earth, white earth, brown earth, we are earth." Her words remind us that we are not separate but bound together—our lives, stories, and responsibilities intertwined. This vision of interconnectedness, reflected in the earth's radiant hues, is not only poetic, it is pedagogical. It mirrors the very heart of *Metacognitive Clarity*, where core elements of learning are not discrete skills to be mastered in isolation, but interwoven threads that strengthen and sustain learning as a living whole. When *purpose*, *process*, and *ownership* align, rigorous thinking becomes democratic work—rooted, like the earth itself, in connection, reciprocity, and care. This book brings that vision to life through three interwoven strands: purpose, process, and ownership.

- **Purpose** (Chapter 5): Just as the earth grounds us in its larger story, clarity of purpose grounds students in meaning. When they see clearly *why* their learning matters, curiosity grows and their sense of belonging is strengthened. When they can connect the work to a larger purpose, their brains light up with interest and care.

- **Process** (Chapter 6): Like paths worn into the soil, process becomes visible when students are shown *how* to learn—how to use strategies, reflect on their progress, and bring their thinking into the open. Making thinking visible is critical to the learning process; learning here becomes intentional.

- **Ownership** (Chapter 7): And as every community flourishes when each member participates, ownership takes shape when students step into agency. This looks like setting goals, assessing growth, and engaging in reflection as active learners. When students take the lead, education shifts from a one-way delivery model into a dynamic dialogue. It is the unboundedness of learning as a shared creation—where voice, choice, and responsibility weave together into something larger than any one individual.

To cultivate a culture of metacognitive clarity is to honor both the interconnectedness that Harjo names and the inner landscapes of learners. It is to see learning not only as content mastery, but as a practice of remembering purpose, refining process, and reclaiming ownership in ways that integrate *who* students are with *what* and *how* they learn. It calls us back to wholeness. And what could be more whole than integrating heart, mind, and community (Chapter 4)? The ideas presented in this text are not theory alone, but a practice that takes shape in relationships, reflection, and the courage to learn (and unlearn) together.

In my former role as a PreK–8th grade principal, I had the pleasure of working with Paul Bloomberg and Isaac Wells at The Core Collaborative. Together, we focused intently on the conditions that liberate thinking (Chapter 3). To make this possible, identity, agency, and belonging (core components of Transformative SEL) became the DNA of our school, and we infused our systems and structures with the principles of metacognitive clarity. Guided by a belief that emotions drive cognition, we focused on what matters: inner landscapes and our collective landscape of community. We looked to the margins and brought every learner and educator into the fabric of the whole. Every lesson, every Impact Team meeting, and every town hall started with operationalizing Brené Brown's call: *"Be here. Be you. Belong."*

During those same years, I also met St. Claire Adriaan, a fellow principal, in a restorative practices session he co-led. Having grown up in South Africa under Apartheid, his lens of justice rooted in community struck me deeply. I knew then his perspective was a rare gift for how to see education as freedom and cultural wealth as its heartbeat. His words on authentic family engagement (Chapter 10) carry that same brilliance, moving me still.

The steady partnership with Paul and Isaac, together with St. Claire's reminder that justice must be rooted in community, shaped a culture where transformation became possible. In collaboration with The Core Collaborative, we advanced democracy by creating classrooms where critical thinking was inseparable from radical care, and where students' voices shaped learning that mattered. Teachers found empowerment in both their instruction and their care for one another. In this culture, thinking and feeling were braided together. Here, democracy was not something to study but something to live—reminding us that schools can be more than places of learning; they can be places of liberation.

The results were striking: doubled test scores, decreased chronic absenteeism, higher teacher retention, and my own growth in learner-centered leadership—culminating in the honor of being named Distinguished Principal of Manhattan. These outcomes left me asking a deeper question: What does it mean to put community at the center and embrace pedagogical and leadership practices that cultivate and sustain belonging? That question became a compass, guiding me into my current role as a Distinguished Lecturer in Educational Leadership studies and the founding director of Social Emotional Learning & Leading (C-SELL) at Hunter College, where I continue to advance metacognitive clarity by building beloved communities across K–12 schools and higher education.

In the final pages of the children's book *Remember*, Harjo extends this invitation, writing:

"Remember the wind. Remember her voice. She knows the origin of this universe. Remember you are all people and all people are you.

Remember all is in motion, is growing, is you.

Remember you are the universe.

And this universe is you.

Remember."

To remember, then, is to reclaim clarity. As Chapter 11 of this text outlines, the future of learning is metacognitive. It is a remembrance that we are part of one another. Seen through the lens of belonging, investing in transformative professional learning (Chapter 9), deepening family engagement, and partnering with consultants at The Core Collaborative might be the most liberating act that you take this school year.

To the dreamers and doers of beloved community and to all who believe that learning can be a pathway to freedom and belonging, I speak to you, and I offer this advice:

- **Step One:** Engage with this text. Hold it with care. Read not just with your eyes, but with your heart and your whole being. As you read, *be* in beloved community with educators, students, and families. This is how a culture of metacognitive clarity takes shape (Chapter 8). Make space for reflection and dialogue. Share what you're learning, and listen for what others carry. Truly, listen. Start a book club at your school. Start a belonging council. Start a metacognitive equity walk. Start a movement. Start small, but start together.

- **Step Two:** Take that leap, as I did as a school leader. Choose to partner with The Core Collaborative. You don't have to do this work alone. Welcome guidance from trusted partners who walk the path with you. In partnership, clarity deepens and metacognitive clarity moves from idea to lived reality.

- **Step Three:** And always return to the ground beneath you. See where you can root into the earth—the same red earth, yellow earth, white earth, brown earth that reminds us our roots hold more than we can see. Root into *purpose*; let it steady your feet. Root into *process*; let it reveal the pathways of learning made visible. Root into *ownership*; let it awaken the agency within. This is the work of metacognitive clarity: *to remember, to root, and to rise*.

Though readers of this text may come from different schools and districts, we belong to one earth, one soil, and one landscape. From this shared ground, our stories intertwine, revealing our shared humanity. And as we lift our eyes to the night sky, our futures connect like constellations—mirroring the cover of this book, where every bright point joins another to form a greater whole. In remembering, we rise, together, as high as the stars.

> "Remember you are the universe. And this universe is you."

Now is the time to reshape what's possible in classrooms. Our charge is clear: to *think rigorously* and to *advance democracy*—across curriculum, within relationships, and throughout systems—so that metacognitive clarity becomes not merely a skill but a way of seeing and being, together, in the universe.

Shine bright.

A LETTER TO OUR READERS

Dear Reader,

You hold a book about learning. *Metacognitive clarity* is our way of naming a simple, radical truth: when learners can name how they are learning, choose strategies that fit, and judge what is working, they do better in school *and* practice the habits that make communities more just and more free. You will find many ideas within the pages of this book, but all of them are tied to two key promises.

Think Rigorously is our first promise.

Rigor lives in the *work learners do with their own thinking*: planning before they begin, monitoring while they work, and adjusting with purpose. It shows up in classrooms when students can say, "Here's my goal . . . here's the strategy I'm trying . . . here's how I know if it's working." Rigor lives in metacognition, where thinking is visible, shared, and coached.

Advance Democracy is our second promise.

Classrooms are communities where we rehearse the civic world. When learners have a voice, co-construct success criteria, engage in peer feedback, and lead parts of the learning cycle, they practice the dispositions a healthy democracy requires: listening for understanding, changing course in light of evidence, and taking responsibility for the whole.

This book is both an invitation and a map.

In **Part I**, we introduce the architecture and conditions that *liberate thinking*—psychological safety, high expectations, and culturally responsive moves that honor identity, language, and lived experience.

In **Part II**, we make the work doable through three anchors you will see again and again:

- **Clarity of Purpose**—*why* this learning matters and how it connects to bigger human pursuits;
- **Clarity of Process**—the *how* of learning-to-learn (planning, monitoring, adjusting, reflecting); and
- **Clarity of Ownership**—who holds the pen and voice along the way.

In **Part III,** we scale the work to whole schools: cultivating culture, growing educator capacity, partnering with families as co-teachers, and navigating a future where artificial intelligence (AI) is everywhere, and humanity must be *even more* intentional about thinking, care, and ethics.

We wrote this for teachers who believe in young people, for leaders who are building cultures of trust and intellectual challenge, and for families who want practical ways to nurture self-directed learners at home. You'll find big ideas, yes, but also routines, protocols, and language you can use tomorrow. The appendix is a toolkit packed with guidance for educators and leaders and K–12 activities you can drop into lessons, advisory periods, intervention blocks, and family nights. Start small and pick one routine, co-construct one set of success criteria, practice one feedback move, and/or gather a little evidence.

Here is our hope for what will grow from these pages:

- Classrooms where students can *name their strategy* and *shift it* when needed.
- Teams that talk about learning with evidence and empathy, not only with grades.
- Families who feel invited into the learning, equipped with simple home moves.
- Schools where students and adults alike become more skilled at noticing, naming, and using thinking in the service of something larger than themselves.

The metacognitive cycle guides us as we make attempts, adjust, and try again. Practiced daily, it becomes a civic habit: we inquire, we listen, we reason, we revise, and we act together.

Thank you for choosing to embark on this journey with us. May it help you grow thinkers who can navigate complexity with courage and kindness, and communities that are a little wiser because those thinkers are in them.

With gratitude, love, and optimism,

Paul, Isaac, and St. Claire

ABOUT THE AUTHORS

Paul J. Bloomberg, EdD

Dr. Paul J. Bloomberg is a Queer educator, national school improvement coach, and best-selling coauthor of *Leading Impact Teams: Building a Culture of Efficacy and Agency*, as well as multiple other books on learner-centered assessment, asset-based pedagogy, and collaborative inquiry. A former principal and district leader, he is the co-creator of the nationally recognized Impact Team School Transformation Model, which has helped schools across the United States and abroad strengthen equity, agency, and collective efficacy. Through The Core Collaborative, the professional learning network he co-founded with his husband, Tony, Dr. Bloomberg has led partnerships with the New York City Department of Education, the United Federation of Teachers, Education Scotland, and the Hawaiʻi Department of Education, among many others. He dedicates this work to their sons, Alex and Taylor, with the mission of ensuring that no child endures the barriers and injustices they faced in school.

Isaac Wells

Isaac Wells is a National Board Certified Teacher, early learning expert, and coauthor of multiple books on learner-centered assessment and student voice. He is also a significant contributor to the best-selling *Leading Impact Teams: Building a Culture of Efficacy and Agency*, second edition. As Director of Impact at The Core Collaborative, Isaac has partnered with schools and systems across the country to embed reflective practices and the metacognitive cycle into daily instruction. His work through The Core Collaborative emphasizes the design of equity-driven systems, where reflection and agency are central to teaching and learning, preparing even the youngest learners for a lifetime of promise and democratic participation.

St. Claire Adriaan, MEd

St. Claire Adriaan is a Harvard graduate, lifelong educator, and coauthor of *Metacognitive Clarity: Think Rigorously. Advance Democracy*. Born and raised in Apartheid South Africa, he experienced education both as a mechanism of oppression and as a pathway to liberation, a perspective that grounds his leadership. Currently principal at PUC CALS in Los Angeles, St. Claire also partners with The Core Collaborative to advance equity-centered leadership and strengthen family–school partnerships nationally. He began his doctoral journey in the fall, continuing his focus on democratic leadership and equity. His work emphasizes whole-child development, democratic participation, and student ownership, ensuring that schools inspire, empower, and prepare young people to lead with clarity and purpose.

HOW TO READ THIS BOOK

This book is both a guide and a companion for your practice. Each chapter introduces key ideas and frameworks for building metacognitive clarity, followed by Reflections and Actions that encourage you to pause, apply, and personalize the learning.

To deepen the experience, you'll also find QR codes that link to short videos—bringing the concepts to life through demonstrations, stories, and practical applications, neuroscience notes to get you thinking about the brain, and call outs to our our online appendices. .

The book unfolds in four interconnected parts:

- **Part I – Vision and Architecture (Introduction and Ch. 1–4):** Frames metacognitive clarity as the through-line between rigorous learning and democratic life, grounding the concept in research (Flavell, Dewey, Freire) and naming the dispositions and conditions that liberate thinking.

- **Part II – Design for Practice (Ch. 5–7):** Operationalizes the work through a highly usable triad—**Clarity of Purpose, Process, and Ownership**—with concrete routines and language educators can use right away.

- **Part III – Systems and Leadership for Metacognitive Clarity (Ch. 8–11 and Closing):** Scales the work outward into culture-building, professional learning, family–school partnerships, and a future-facing chapter that situates metacognition in an AI-inflected world.

- **Part IV – Appendices:** Offers ready-to-use tools, protocols, and classroom learning experiences across K–12 content areas, so you can see how metacognitive clarity looks in practice at every level. For ease of use, the downloadable PDF appendices are organized into five sections: Clarity of Purpose, Clarity of Process, Clarity of Ownership, Leadership and Implementation Support, and General Resources. This structure makes it simple to locate the roles, resources, and strategies you need.

You can choose to read the book straight through to follow the arc of ideas, or dip into specific chapters, tools, and videos as your needs arise. However you approach it, let the rhythm of ideas, reflection, and action guide you toward building clarity—for yourself, your students, and your community.

Metacognition increases rigor by deepening students' engagement and cognitive complexity in learning tasks. Here's how:

1. **Promotes Deeper Thinking:**
   Metacognition pushes learners beyond surface-level recall by encouraging them to

analyze, question, and evaluate their own thought processes. This active reflection leads students to grapple with complex concepts rather than passively consuming information.

2. **Enhances Problem-Solving:**
Students who think metacognitively learn to approach problems methodically. They articulate their strategies, monitor their progress, and adapt as needed—resulting in more sophisticated problem-solving skills.

3. **Builds Transferable Skills:**
Metacognitive awareness helps students recognize patterns and connections across content areas. This transferability ensures that learners apply their understanding to novel situations, significantly elevating academic rigor.

4. **Encourages Self-Directed Learning:**
Learners who set goals, self-monitor, and adjust their learning strategies become more autonomous. They challenge themselves to meet higher standards because they internalize accountability and high expectations.

5. **Supports Critical Reflection and Evaluation:**
Metacognition prompts learners to assess their own performance and understanding critically. By regularly evaluating the quality of their learning, students push themselves toward deeper understanding and more rigorous standards.

In essence, metacognition turns learning from passive reception into active exploration, significantly raising the level of rigor in the classroom.

Neuroscience Notes

When you see this icon, you can expect tidbits about the brain and what we know about how learning happens. We hope these notes will get you thinking and spark your interest while also providing additional support to the ideas shared in each chapter.

Online Appendices

This icon is a reminder to visit the resources available at: (as well as by scanning the QR code below). The password is ***Democracy*** combining two of the key concepts from the book and, we hope, making it easy to remember.

PART I:
VISION AND ARCHITECTURE

INTRODUCTION

At its core, learning is an exercise in democracy.

Metacognitive Clarity: A New Vision for Learning

Some readers may find this idea surprising. For generations, we've accepted a model of education where teachers deliver information, and students passively receive it. Historically, this teacher-centered paradigm, grounded in explicit instruction and measurable outcomes, has informed our educational policies and practices for many years. It carries the implicit assumption of a power dynamic in which teachers exert complete control over student learning. While there is no question that teachers play an essential role in student learning, this book takes the position that, given the right tools and conditions, students must actively construct their own understanding in partnership with their teachers, not only of academic content but also of themselves and the world around them.

Metacognition, defined by Flavell (1979) as "the active monitoring and consequent regulation and orchestration" of one's cognitive processes (p. 232), invites us to reconsider the teacher-centered paradigm. Metacognitive clarity transforms traditional notions of "teacher clarity" from mere transmission of explicit instruction to an active, student-centered practice grounded in democracy, equity, justice, and self-determination. Teachers explicitly model and implement the metacognitive cycle across all subjects—planning, monitoring, and evaluating—to help students internalize and master these essential skills. This intentional modeling empowers learners to actively reflect on their cognitive processes, shaping meaningful learning journeys that connect deeply with their identities, communities, and broader societal contexts.

Figure I.1: The Metacognitive Cycle

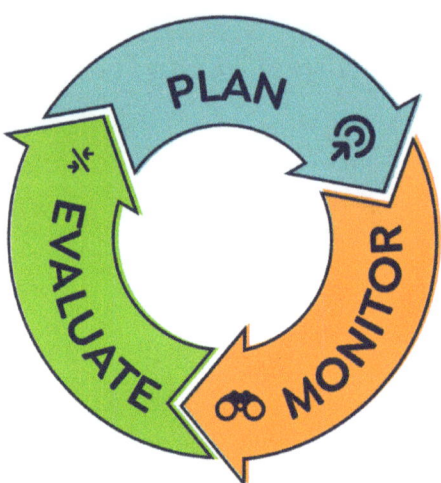

PLAN
- Set a clear goal
- Analyze a model
- Co-construct success criteria
- Choose strategies and tools
- Schedule checkpoints

MONITOR
- Check against success criteria
- Collect quick evidence
- Use self-talk or partner feedback
- Adjust strategies, time, or supports

EVALUATE
- Compare final work to success criteria/model
- Name what strategies/conditions worked and why
- Identify growth and needs
- Set next steps: revise, practice, or extend

Through systematic teaching of reflective strategies and critical self-awareness, metacognitive clarity empowers all students, irrespective of background or identity, to thoughtfully and confidently navigate their educational experiences. Central to this is learner agency, the capacity and willingness of students to take purposeful initiative, ownership, and accountability for their learning. By fostering learner agency, metacognitive clarity cultivates empathy, equity, and active democratic participation.

While teachers play a significant role in nurturing metacognitive clarity, their efforts are significantly amplified when they work in partnership with students' families. Families are a significant influence on learners' identities, beliefs about learning, and sense of agency and belonging. When families are intentionally and authentically engaged, they amplify the impact of metacognitive strategies and contribute deeply to equitable educational outcomes. By actively co-constructing goals, monitoring progress, and reflecting alongside educators and students, families become crucial allies in democratic, justice-driven education. For an in-depth exploration of how family–school partnerships reinforce and sustain metacognitive clarity, learner agency, and equity, refer to Chapter 10 of this book: "Amplifying Metacognitive Clarity Through Family–School Partnerships."

From Teacher Clarity to Metacognitive Clarity

Many readers are, no doubt, familiar with the concept of Teacher Clarity—a practice employed by teachers that involves setting clear learning goals, sharing them with students, and using success criteria to guide both instruction and assessment. The concept has its roots in the work of pioneering educational psychologists of the 1980s (Berliner, 1986; Rosenshine & Stevens, 1986) but was more recently popularized by researcher John Hattie (2012). The term has long been recognized as a powerful influence on student learning; however, Hattie's extensive research helped underscore just how powerful an impact it exerts. Based on the findings of numerous meta-analyses, Hattie assigned a teacher clarity effect size of 0.75, nearly 90% higher than the average rate of progress. Hattie and others attest to the power of teacher clarity for reducing cognitive load and laying a foundation for formative assessment.

What is striking in the traditional conceptualization of teacher clarity (and the teacher-centered paradigm in general) is that it is commonly framed as something we "do to students." While we won't dispute its importance, we propose shifting beyond the traditional teacher clarity concept toward what we call metacognitive clarity. Imagine a learning environment where students are not merely recipients of explicit instruction but actively engaged participants who deeply understand why their learning matters. Flavell (1979) states that metacognition involves "the active monitoring and consequent regulation and orchestration" of one's own cognitive processes (p. 232). Metacognitive clarity emphasizes learners' intentional engagement in planning their learning paths, continuously monitoring progress, and evaluating outcomes.

This shift to metacognitive clarity transforms traditional conceptualizations of clarity to collective, democratic practices. It ensures that learning is deeply relevant to each student's identity, experiences, and aspirations. Metacognitive equity, central to this approach, guarantees every student, irrespective of background, language, or identity, has the essential tools to critically engage, monitor their growth, and actively pursue their goals. Importantly, metacognition supports not only cognitive development but also social and emotional learning. It connects deeply with every dimension of learning, enabling students to better understand themselves, manage their emotions, empathize with others, and engage meaningfully with their communities.

At a time when artificial intelligence is transforming how knowledge is produced, and misinformation spreads faster than truth, the stakes of education have changed. Students no longer just need to retain information; they must learn to question, evaluate, and discern. Metacognitive clarity equips learners with the reflective tools to navigate complexity, resist manipulation, and engage ethically in a world of accelerated change. This work is about discerning fact from fiction, safeguarding democracy, and improving learning.

By nurturing metacognitive clarity, we empower students to actively shape their futures, rather than simply comply, to truly embrace education as an act of democratic justice.

The Call for Metacognitive Equity

Metacognitive equity demands universal access to skills in self-awareness, self-regulation, and critical thinking. As Bloomberg et al. (2023) emphasize in *Amplify Learner Voice Through Culturally Responsive and Sustaining Assessment*, metacognitive strategies are tools of equity that must be made accessible to all learners, including those who have been historically underserved by a sorting system that privileges answers over reflection.

When we explicitly teach metacognition to all students, we model essential skills for navigating an increasingly complex and ambiguous world. We also serve as agents of justice. When learners master skills to plan, monitor, and evaluate their thinking, they gain control over their educational journeys and futures.

Metacognitive teaching must be universal:

- **Multilingual learners** must leverage their linguistic and cultural strengths through reflective practices that affirm their identities, deepen their self-awareness, and foster intercultural competence and collaboration.
- **Students with disabilities** should harness strategies that celebrate neurodiversity; honor varied ways of knowing, thinking, and learning; and promote autonomy through individualized, reflective, and adaptive approaches.
- **Students historically marginalized** by systemic inequities must experience metacognition as empowerment, resilience, advocacy, and leadership, recognizing their lived experiences as assets contributing uniquely to their reflective and critical capacities.
- **All students** must develop metacognitive skills as a universal pathway for building empathy, self-awareness, personal responsibility, and collaborative leadership, preparing them to engage meaningfully and thoughtfully with diverse peers and communities.

No learner's access to these critical cognitive processes should depend on identities, perceived ability, or ZIP code. Metacognitive equity means valuing every voice and trusting every learner to drive their growth.

The Metacognitive Cycle

The metacognitive cycle is adaptive and iterative:

- **Plan:** Activate prior knowledge, set meaningful goals, and anticipate challenges.
- **Monitor:** Track progress, adjust strategies, and manage emotions.
- **Evaluate:** Reflect on outcomes, assess strategies, and plan future steps.

You already do this. Any time you plan a meal, monitor the budget while shopping, and evaluate how dinner went, you're running Plan–Monitor–Evaluate. The point isn't to add one more thing to anyone's plate—it's to *name and sharpen* what parents and caregivers, families, students, educators, and leaders already do in daily life. When people recognize their existing strategies, they adopt and refine them faster—at home, in classrooms, and in teams.

By explicitly modeling and consistently reinforcing the metacognitive cycle, educators not only guide students in developing lifelong habits of reflective learning but also empower them to navigate their learning processes independently. In doing so, students build the capacity to help themselves by transforming into self-sufficient, reflective learners who can confidently adapt and grow throughout their lives. Simultaneously, this practice invites educators to lean into their own humanity—deepening their self-awareness and understanding of their thinking, biases, and growth areas—and ultimately fostering a more authentic, empathetic connection with their students.

Metacognitive Clarity in Action

To achieve metacognitive clarity, educators must intentionally design learning experiences grounded in justice, democracy, and student agency. Learning experiences must have:

- **Clarity of Purpose:** Learning goals must be deeply tied to identity, community, and social justice. (Chapter 5)
- **Clarity of Process:** Students learn adaptable strategies that respect their diverse cognitive strengths. (Chapter 6)
- **Clarity of Ownership:** Students regularly co-create success criteria, self-assess, and reflect, ensuring meaningful ownership. (Chapter 7)

Classrooms that embrace metacognitive clarity become democratic spaces, where dialogue, questioning, and collective reasoning are celebrated.

What Does the Evidence Say?

The journey to understand and harness the power of metacognition spans centuries and cultures, illuminating its essential role across diverse educational contexts. From Indigenous educational practices globally to foundational explorations by John Flavell in the 1970s, scholars have continually expanded our understanding of metacognition. Recent research further integrates equity and culturally responsive practices, empowering learners to actively engage with their cognitive processes. The timeline below highlights key milestones, bridging historical insights with contemporary innovations.

Global Roots and Contemporary Development of Metacognition

Metacognition has deep historical roots, evident long before colonial influence. However, it is often discussed through contemporary research and academic language, a framing that can obscure the fact that many Indigenous and global communities have long cultivated practices that support reflection, self-regulation, and purposeful action as part of everyday learning and life. Acknowledging these foundations is essential to understanding metacognition in ways that honor culture, context, and human experience. The following timeline situates current theory within this broader human context, honoring Indigenous ways of knowing while tracing how metacognition came to be formally named, studied, and applied in education.

Precolonial to Present: Indigenous Foundations

- **North America:** Navajo, Ojibwe, and Lakota tribes used storytelling, reflective dialogue, and experiential learning (Cajete, 1994; Barnhardt & Kawagley, 2005).
- **Hawaiʻi:** Native Hawaiians emphasized reflective, experiential learning through apprenticeships with kahuna (experts), storytelling (moʻolelo), chants (oli), dances (hula), and place-based practices (aloha ʻāina), cultivating deep self-awareness and adaptive learning strategies (Alencastre & Kawaiʻaeʻa, 2018).
- **Australia:** Aboriginal peoples integrated Dreamtime stories and reflective observation to deepen cognitive awareness (Yunkaporta, 2019).
- **Africa:** Yoruba and Akan communities utilized proverbs, storytelling, and communal reflection for strategic problem-solving (Wiredu, 2004).
- **Asia:** The Ainu of Japan embedded oral traditions and reflective practices into educational methods (Irimoto, 2004).

1900s: Conceptual Foundations

- **1910:** John Dewey's concept of reflective thinking refers to an intentional, active, and persistent examination of one's beliefs, ideas, experiences, and actions to deepen understanding and improve future decisions (1910).
- **1966:** Jerome Bruner, in *Toward a Theory of Instruction* (1966), underscores the active role educators play in stimulating learners' thinking, setting the stage for later explorations into metacognition.
- **1976:** John Flavell introduces "metacognition," defining metacognitive knowledge and regulation (Flavell, 1976).
- **1977:** Ann Brown expands concepts, emphasizing the importance of monitoring and controlling cognitive strategies (Brown, 1977).

1980s: Educational Applications and Development

- **1981:** Brown et al. highlight metacognitive skills essential for reading comprehension and problem-solving in learners (Brown et al., 1981).
- **1985:** Developmental progression of metacognition in children is detailed, embedding metacognition firmly into educational psychology (Flavell et al., 1985).

1990s: Classroom Integration and Measurement

- **1992:** Paris and Winograd (1992) link metacognition directly to intrinsic motivation and academic success.
- **1994:** Schraw and Dennison (1994) create the Metacognitive Awareness Inventory (MAI), standardizing measurement and classroom integration.

2000s: Neurological Insights and Self-Regulation

- **2002:** Pintrich (2002) integrates metacognition with self-regulated learning models, underscoring learner autonomy.
- **2005:** Nelson and Narens (1990) differentiate between cognitive monitoring and control.
- **2012:** Neuroscience identifies brain regions (e.g., prefrontal cortex) associated with metacognition (Fleming & Dolan, 2012).

2010s: Comprehensive Research and Neuroscience Expansion

- **2010:** Hattie's (2010) synthesis "Visible Learning" identifies significant educational impacts of metacognitive strategies (effect size ~0.69).
- **2011–2012:** Efklides (2011) introduces the Metacognitive and Affective Model of Self-Regulated Learning (MASRL), integrating emotions, motivation, and metacognition.
- **2022:** Neuroscience further clarifies neurological correlates of metacognition, confirming the central role of executive brain functions (Boldt & Gilbert, 2022).

2015 to Present: Equity, Cultural Contexts, and Pedagogical Innovation

- **2015:** Hammond (2015) promotes culturally responsive teaching and equity-focused metacognitive strategies.
- **2018:** Quigley, Muijs, and Stringer (2018) demonstrate that metacognitive interventions effectively address disparities in disadvantaged learners.
- **2020–2021:** Ambrose et al. (2010) and Muhammad align metacognitive pedagogies with culturally affirming, neuroscience-informed strategies.

This timeline illustrates the evolution of metacognition, tracing its roots from Indigenous global foundations through rigorous academic development and contemporary practices that prioritize equity and culturally responsive teaching. These collective insights continue shaping inclusive and effective educational strategies worldwide.

Nurturing and Sustaining Democracy

Metacognitive clarity is a moral imperative. It asks us to enhance and fundamentally transform learning as we engage in continuous improvement. We titled this book with two carefully chosen maxims: *Think Rigorously. Advance Democracy.* As you work through the following chapters and related resources, you will see how metacognitive clarity enables learners of all ages to do both.

Rigorous thinking is not about doing more work or harder work. It is about engaging deeply, reflectively, and responsibly with ideas. It requires learners to question assumptions, evaluate evidence, consider multiple perspectives, and connect their thinking to real-world contexts. Rigorous thinking also reflects a balanced approach to learning, encouraging surface understanding, deep reasoning, and meaningful transfer, so that students not only know content but can also apply it in new situations. In our schools, rigorous thinking mirrors the habits of a thriving democracy: listening respectfully, weighing different viewpoints, and making reasoned decisions that balance individual rights with collective responsibility.

This definition aligns with McDowell's (2024) emphasis that high-quality teaching balances knowing, connecting, and applying core knowledge—linking surface, deep, and transfer learning in support of student ownership of learning.

Democracy, in the context of learning, is both a structure and a practice. A thriving school community, like a healthy democracy, depends on shared values, mutual respect, and the participation of everyone. The same principles on which our country was founded can guide how we learn, lead, and grow together. Schools must intentionally build the structures that ask students to participate meaningfully and make impactful decisions, and this practice must become commonplace. By living these ideals and taking an active role in shaping education for themselves and their peers at school, we prepare every student for a lifetime of active citizenship.

Principles of Democracy in Our Learning Community

(Inspired by the Declaration of Independence, the U.S. Constitution, and the Bill of Rights)

Shared Voice and Choice (Popular Sovereignty): Just as government draws its power from the people, our school thrives when students, families, and staff have a say in shaping learning and community decisions.

Everyone Follows the Same Rules (Rule of Law): We all follow agreed-upon norms and policies, ensuring fairness and safety for every member of the school community.

Different Roles, Shared Purpose (Separation of Powers): Like the branches of government, students, teachers, administrators, and families each have unique responsibilities that work together toward our shared mission.

Balancing Responsibilities (Checks and Balances): We hold one another accountable, ensuring that power and responsibility are shared and that everyone is treated with respect.

Rights and Freedoms for All (Individual Rights): Every student and staff member has the right to express their ideas, practice their culture, and be themselves while honoring the rights of others.

Fairness and Inclusion (Equality Under the Law): Every member of our school is valued and included, with equal access to opportunities and support.

Respectful Processes (Due Process): Decisions are made fairly and consistently, and everyone has the chance to share their side of the story.

Contributing to Our Community (Civic Responsibility): We all work to make our school a better place by helping others, solving problems together, and making choices that benefit the whole community.

Our Civic Empowerment Reflection Cards and Democratic Dialogue Circle guidance are two examples of how to bring these democratic principles to life in the classroom. Find both in the Learning Tools for Clarity of Purpose under heading Purpose-Driven Reflection and Action how you can adapt them in your school.

In the chapters that follow, we explore how learners build metacognitive clarity across purpose, process, and ownership. In Chapter 6, we examine how students develop adaptive thinking strategies to manage distraction, navigate emotional responses, and reflect on their learning in real time. These routines become essential in today's complex landscape, especially as we explore in Chapter 10 the rising influence of artificial intelligence and misinformation. In a world where truth is contested and technology rapidly reshapes society, metacognitive clarity equips students to learn, discern, question, and act with integrity. It is this kind of clarity that prepares students to engage powerfully in both their classrooms and their communities.

Reflect and Act

When we embed metacognitive clarity into everyday instructional practices, we nurture a robust learner identity grounded in agency, reflection, and democratic participation. Of course, the process begins with us—the adults in the room. We grow our own metacognitive capacities by intentionally planning, monitoring, and evaluating how students think about their thinking. Instructional teams create classrooms where every voice is valued, particularly those of emergent bilinguals, students with disabilities, and traditionally marginalized groups. This reflective, actionable approach ensures that metacognition becomes a powerful tool—not just for learning, but for fostering a deep, inclusive sense of community, equity, and democratic engagement.

Plan

- Determine concrete steps your instructional teams will take to universally embed the metacognitive cycle (Plan, Monitor, Evaluate) as an everyday practice, explicitly connecting it to learner identity and democratic engagement.
- Create action plans to ensure equitable access to metacognitive strategies for all students, focusing on emergent bilinguals, students with disabilities, and traditionally marginalized groups.

Monitor

- Regularly assess how effectively you and your peers integrate metacognitive practices aligned with democratic principles of agency, voice, and collective decision-making.
- Continuously collect and analyze student reflections, feedback, and progress indicators to monitor engagement, empowerment, and the inclusivity of metacognitive instruction.

Evaluate

- Conduct periodic evaluations of the influence of metacognitive clarity on student achievement, sense of identity, and democratic participation. Identify key strengths and areas for growth.
- Host collaborative, reflective dialogues among students, educators, and leadership teams to critically evaluate and refine the ongoing application of metacognitive clarity, reinforcing a shared vision of justice, equity, and learner agency.

CHAPTER 1

THE ARCHITECTURE OF METACOGNITIVE CLARITY

Learning is not a purely cognitive activity.
It is inseparably tied to identity, belonging, and meaning.
— **Zaretta Hammond**

Clarity is essential in every thriving community, whether on the ancient streets of Athens or in the vibrant classrooms of today. Think of clarity as the unseen scaffolding upon which transformative learning is built. Yet, as we suggested in the Introduction, traditional approaches to "teacher clarity" are transactional and even undemocratic in nature; they presuppose a teacher-centered dynamic in which educators "spoon-feed" clarity by explicitly communicating learning intentions, and students passively receive it. But what if clarity is something that teachers and students co-construct, something that we build together?

Imagine for a moment a classroom where clarity is a human right. In such spaces, students become architects of their educational journeys. According to Gholdy Muhammad (2021), authentic clarity empowers students to co-create knowledge, aligning their learning deeply with who they are and who they aspire to become. When we approach clarity this way, education becomes an act of democracy and liberation (Hammond, 2015).

Learner Identity: The Cornerstone of Metacognitive Clarity

While there are many definitions of "identity," its essential meaning can be captured in a deceptively simple question: "Who am I?" The question may seem simple enough on the surface, but it invites a plethora of complex, highly nuanced responses. The influential psychologist and educator Beverly Daniels Tatum explains why:

> The answer depends in large part on who the world around me says I am. Who do my parents say I am? Who do my peers say I am? What message is reflected back to me in the faces and voices of my teachers, my neighbors, and store clerks? What do I learn from the media about myself? How am I represented in the cultural images around me? Or am I missing from the picture altogether? (Tatum, 2000)

The term *social identity* refers to our sense of self in the context of groups to which we belong (and those to which we *don't* belong, for that matter). Social identities include race, ethnicity, gender, religion, nationality, language, and sexuality. *Personal identity*, in contrast, reflects who we are as individuals. Examples might include generous, creative, and introverted. Great teachers intentionally acknowledge, affirm, and celebrate both the social and personal identities of their students.

For example, a math teacher who integrates students' cultural practices, like weaving patterns from Indigenous communities, connects mathematics directly to their lived experiences. Or imagine a literature class where students share personal narratives that parallel the texts they read—an activity that affirms diverse perspectives and fosters a powerful sense of belonging and validation.

In the context of metacognitive clarity, one's learner identity is particularly significant. Learner identity refers to how students see themselves as learners. The construction of a learner identity is influenced by a student's beliefs, values, experiences, and perceptions. Why is learner identity so essential? Because how students see themselves profoundly shapes their motivation, persistence, and engagement in school and beyond. Learner identity isn't a fixed trait. It evolves continuously, influenced by relationships, culture, community, and experiences. It encompasses beliefs about capability, feelings toward learning, behaviors, and awareness of thought processes. And it encompasses aspects of both social and personal identities. For example, a student might disclose, "I'm good at math but not good at solving word problems." The same student might be a multilingual learner who has been labeled "English learner," a socially constructed category that contributes to a negative learner identity.

Learner identity evolves continuously through interactions with educators, peers, and especially families—key partners who significantly shape students' beliefs about their abilities and learning potential. Building strong family–school partnerships reinforces positive learner identities and ensures alignment between home and school environments. For a deeper exploration of family engagement strategies that amplify learner identity and metacognitive clarity, see Chapter 10: "Amplifying Metacognitive Clarity Through Family–School Partnerships."

Identity and Learning Are Neurologically Linked

When students connect learning to who they are, the medial prefrontal cortex—a brain region involved in self-referential thinking and personal meaning-making—is activated, helping them process information in more meaningful ways. This strengthens memory, motivation, and engagement (Lieberman, 2013; Marcus et al., 2020). Educators who understand and nurture positive learner identities are able to tailor learning experiences that help students feel valued, capable, and connected. By intentionally recognizing and affirming each student's unique strengths, interests, and experiences, educators foster an environment where deeper learning and meaningful personal growth thrive.

Here are concrete examples of strategies educators use to support positive learner identities:

- **Interest-Based Projects:** Incorporating students' personal interests, such as a passion for animals, into curriculum units (e.g., student-led research on animal habitats), affirming students' identities and driving deeper engagement.
- **Asset-Based Feedback:** Providing feedback that emphasizes students' linguistic and cultural strengths rather than only their mistakes (e.g., highlighting a multilingual learner's

rich vocabulary in multiple languages), building their confidence, and reinforcing their capability.

- **Classroom Identity Maps:** Beginning the year with identity-mapping activities—where students visually represent their personal values, experiences, and aspirations—and then consistently referencing these maps in daily learning, enhancing feelings of connection and belonging.
- **Flexible Demonstrations of Learning:** Offering students choices in how they demonstrate their understanding—such as essays, podcasts, or visual art projects—aligning assessments with their individual strengths, fostering students' sense of agency and capability.
- **Restorative Circles and Social-Emotional Learning (SEL) Practices:** Facilitating regular community-building circles to support open dialogue on emotions, relationships, and community issues, ensuring every student feels connected, safe, and valued.
- **Goal Setting and Self-Assessment:** Guiding students to set personalized SMART (Specific, Measurable, Achievable, Relevant, and Time-bound) goals and engage in regular reflection and self-assessment, empowering students to take ownership of their growth and reinforcing their sense of capability and accomplishment.

When educators consistently implement these approaches, they create conditions that cultivate positive learner identities, which in turn promote deeper, lasting learning and personal empowerment. Think of learner identity as a mosaic—multidimensional and culturally textured:

- **Self-Efficacy:** belief in one's own capabilities
- **Belonging:** feeling included and valued
- **Agency and Autonomy:** control over one's learning path
- **Academic Mindset:** beliefs about learning itself
- **Cultural Intersectionality:** the complex interplay of various identities shaping experiences and perspectives

The Learner Agency Tree

One way to visualize this multidimensional construction of learner identity is through the Learner Agency Tree (see Figures 1.1 and 1.2). The roots represent cultural identity, consisting of the deep histories, languages, and traditions that nourish all learning. The trunk symbolizes learner identity, including the beliefs, mindsets, and dispositions that shape how students see themselves as capable learners. From this sturdy center, branches and leaves emerge as academic competencies and literacies, while the fruit represents the contributions and future possibilities learners bring to their communities. Throughout this book, we return to the image of the tree as a guiding metaphor. In Chapter 9, we will explore the Learner Agency Tree in depth, considering how educators can intentionally cultivate the conditions for strong roots, a resilient trunk, and flourishing branches.

Table 1.1 provides examples of how teachers might work to elevate each of these components of learner identity.

Table 1.1: Understanding the Components of Learner Identity

Component	Definition	Teacher Example
Self-Efficacy	Belief in one's own capabilities	A teacher provides specific, timely feedback highlighting students' strengths and improvements, fostering their belief in their own abilities.
Belonging	Feeling included and valued	A teacher regularly conducts community-building circles, where students share personal stories, promoting empathy and inclusivity.
Agency and Autonomy	Control over one's learning path	Students are invited to set personal learning goals and choose from multiple paths or projects to demonstrate their understanding.
Academic Mindset	Beliefs about learning itself	A teacher explicitly teaches growth mindset strategies, reinforcing that intelligence and skills can be developed through effort.
Cultural Intersectionality	The complex interplay of various identities shapes experiences and perspectives	A teacher incorporates diverse literature and histories into lessons, encouraging students to explore and share how their identities influence their views and understandings.

When educators intentionally nurture these facets of learner identity, students thrive in school and beyond. Research indicates that fostering positive learner identities enhances students' intrinsic motivation, deepens their engagement, and promotes effective self-regulation (Nasir & Hand, 2008; Oyserman & Destin, 2010; Yeager & Dweck, 2012). Students become more resilient and persistent through challenges because their learning experiences authentically resonate with their true selves (Gholson & Martin, 2019).

Figure 1.1: Learner Agency Tree Key

**FRUIT:
CONTRIBUTION**

Inquire
Innovate
Engage
Advocate
Create
Teach

**BRANCHES:
CORE COMPETENCIES**

Critical Thinking
Metacognition
Communication
Collaboration
Digital Literacy
Creativity & Adaptability

**TRUNK:
LEARNER IDENTITY**

Collaboration
Perseverance
Reflection
Empathy
Courage
Curiosity

**ROOTS:
CULTURAL IDENTITY**

Belonging
Heritage
Family & Traditions
Values & Beliefs
Ways of Knowing
Home Language

Figure 1.2: Learner Agency Tree

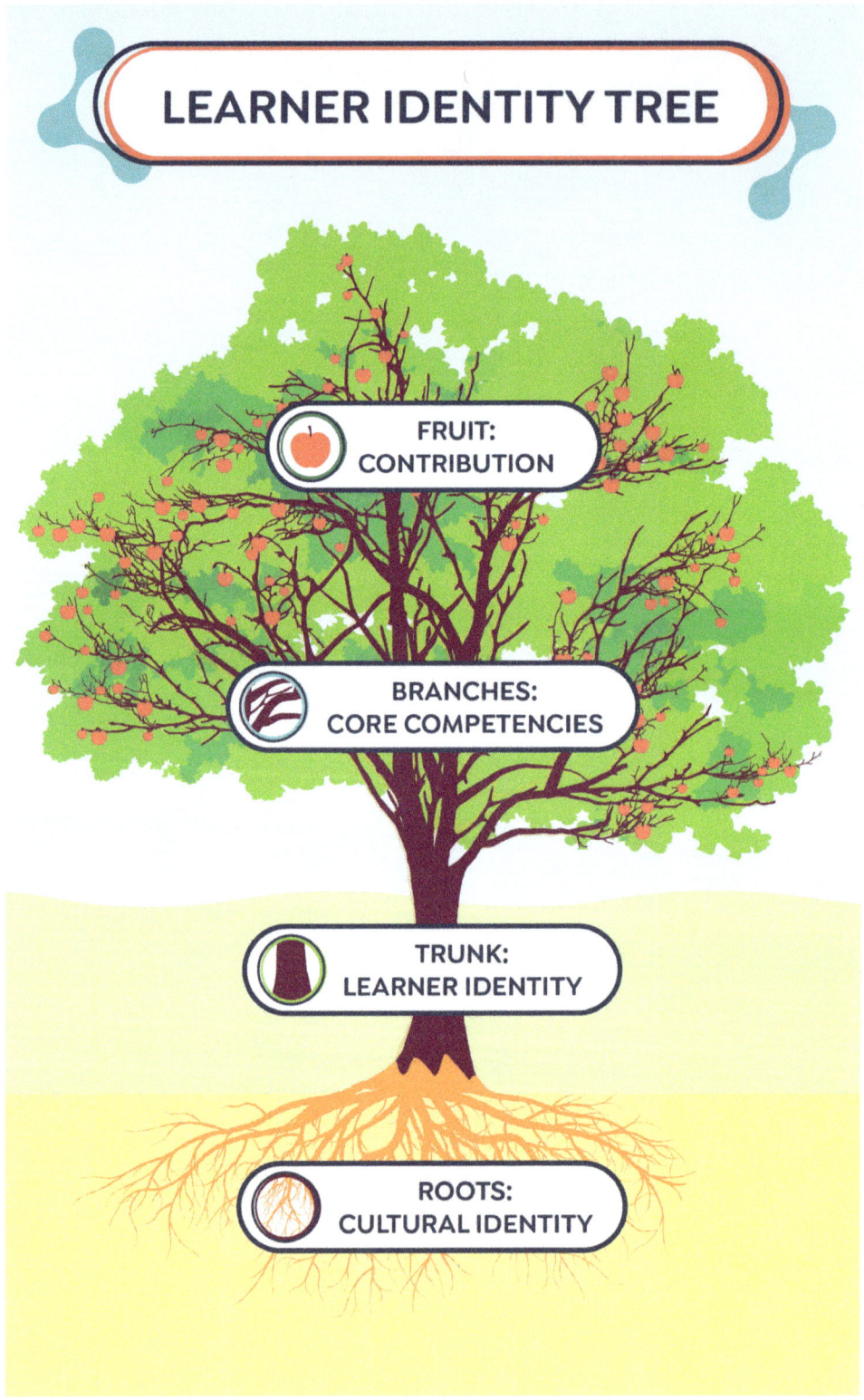

Reflecting on Your Own Learner Identity:

- **Identity and Learning:** How do my personal and social identities shape the way I approach new learning or professional challenges?
- **Beliefs about Capability:** What beliefs do I hold about my abilities in areas I find difficult, and how do these beliefs influence my growth as a learner?
- **Sense of Belonging:** In which learning spaces or subject areas do I feel most valued, included, and connected—and why?
- **Learner Agency:** When have I felt most empowered and in control of my learning, and what conditions supported this experience?

Refer to the *Identity and Belonging Integration Checklist* in the Learning Tools for Clarity of Purpose under the heading *Identity, Justice, and Belonging as Foundations* for a tool that will support you and your team in connecting learning with students' identities.

Metacognition and Learner Identity

Learner identity is the cornerstone upon which authentic metacognition is built. When educators intentionally nurture learner identity, they create the conditions necessary for deep, reflective learning rooted in genuine self-awareness. For example, a math teacher who notices a student's math anxiety might take steps to elevate that student's math learner identity, such as normalizing mistakes as natural learning opportunities and using strengths-based language like "you are developing your mathematical thinking."

Metacognition, or the act of reflecting on one's thinking processes, becomes truly powerful when students can connect their learning experiences to their sense of self. This is because identity informs how learners perceive their capabilities, shape their goals, and interpret their experiences. Students who clearly understand and embrace their learner identities are better equipped to monitor their progress, adapt strategies, and persist through challenges, while contributing meaningfully to culturally affirming and justice-oriented learning communities.

Here's why learner identity matters so deeply to metacognition:

- **Personal Relevance:** Students reflect deeply when learning is personally meaningful.
- **Agency and Self-Regulation:** Identity clarity empowers goal-setting, strategic monitoring, and adaptable thinking.
- **Motivation and Persistence:** A strong learner identity helps students navigate setbacks as opportunities for growth.
- **Cultural Connection:** Identity and metacognition flourish in communities where reflective dialogue is the norm.
- **Equity and Justice:** Authentic reflection depends on students seeing themselves genuinely represented in their educational experiences.

Metacognition without learner identity is hollow. True reflection emerges from understanding oneself deeply within the learning context.

The Core Elements of Metacognitive Clarity

Metacognitive clarity is supported by three interconnected pillars that you may recall from the Introduction:

- **Clarity of Purpose:** Knowing why learning matters beyond the classroom. (This pillar is covered in greater depth in Chapter 5 of this book.)
- **Clarity of Process:** Having clear strategies to navigate learning effectively. (Chapter 6)
- **Clarity of Ownership:** Actively co-creating and owning learning experiences. (Chapter 7)

The whole of this process is greater than the sum of the parts. Purpose gives learning direction, process provides actionable strategies, and ownership ensures sustained engagement and meaningful transfer (Efklides, 2012).

From Surface Clarity to Metacognitive Inquiry

Like content standards, the traditional approach to teacher clarity emphasizes surface-level knowledge: Its primary outcome is to provide students with a clear understanding of *what* they need to know. Metacognitive clarity, in contrast, encourages deeper inquiry by pushing students to consistently explore beyond the surface—to question the underlying purpose ("why"), examine processes and strategies ("how"), and anticipate next steps ("what now?"). This intentional shift transforms how learners engage across disciplines.

Consider how this shift transforms disciplines:

- **English Language Arts:** From identifying themes to exploring how these themes reflect and challenge students' lived realities, personal identities, and societal roles.
- **Math:** From solving problems to reflecting strategically on problem-solving methods, assessing efficiency, and considering alternative approaches.
- **Science:** From memorizing cycles to investigating local ecosystem impacts, prompting questions about environmental justice and community sustainability.
- **Social Studies:** From knowing historical facts to critically examining whose stories are told, whose perspectives are missing, and how history shapes contemporary societal issues.
- **Arts:** From learning artistic techniques to questioning how artistic expression reflects cultural identities, communicates social messages, and challenges societal norms.
- **Music:** From performing compositions to analyzing how music conveys emotions, embodies cultural histories, and influences social movements and personal experiences.
- **Physical Education:** From mastering physical skills to understanding how movement and teamwork strategies contribute to personal wellness, collective efficacy, and cultural traditions.

Through metacognitive inquiry, students become active participants in their learning, building deeper, more reflective connections across all disciplines. When metacognitive clarity is prioritized in every subject area across an entire school, students are driven less by extrinsic rewards, such as getting good grades, and more by their self-driven desire to learn. Students who are internally motivated are more likely to become self-regulated learners who set goals, monitor their progress, and reflect on their learning (Paris & Winograd, 1992).

The Architecture Is Collaborative

Clarity isn't built in isolation. It emerges through collective reflection, dialogue, and purposeful collaboration. Unlike traditional professional learning communities (PLCs) that focus solely on educator collaboration, the Impact Team Collaborative Inquiry Model is the only PLC model that intentionally partners with students to build learner agency. Rather than completing tasks in isolation, students co-construct learning intentions, success criteria, and assessments alongside their teachers. Within this model, trust, empathy, and shared purpose aren't just byproducts—they're foundational elements of a living, vibrant learning community.

Impact Teams (Bloomberg & Pitchford, 2023) bring educators and students together in meaningful partnerships to analyze evidence of learning, set shared goals, and engage in cycles of reflective inquiry. These collaborative teams elevate student voice and agency by making student thinking visible and central to instructional decisions. Through consistent, structured dialogue around authentic learning evidence, students and teachers work side-by-side to identify strengths, address challenges, and co-develop strategies that advance metacognitive clarity.

One of the most powerful tools Impact Teams use is the Analysis of Evidence (AOE) Protocol, which integrates the metacognitive cycle into each phase of inquiry. Table 1.2 illustrates how evidence, analysis, and action are guided by planning, monitoring, evaluating, and acting prompts, which ensures clarity and intentionality at every stage.

Table 1.2: Analysis of Evidence (AOE) Protocol

Phase	Goal	Metacognitive Prompts
Evidence	Gather the proper evidence anchored in clarity of purpose.	**Planning:** What evidence do we need to answer our learning question? **Monitoring:** Are the rubric/targets/success criteria clearly visible? Have we included student work (with code names) and, if possible, perception or self-assessment data? **Evaluating:** Does this evidence give us an accurate, fair, and comprehensive picture of student learning? What might be missing? **Acting:** Collect and organize the evidence so it's ready for analysis.
Analysis	Identify patterns of strengths and needs across students.	**Planning:** What success criteria will we use as anchors for analysis? **Monitoring:** As we sort evidence, are we noticing consistency across student groups or outliers? **Evaluating:** What patterns emerge in student strengths? Where are misconceptions most common? Are students at surface, deep, or transfer levels? **Acting:** Summarize findings in a table by code name and place students into performance bands (e.g., Beginning, Developing, Proficient, Advanced).
Action	Design instructional responses that are targeted, equitable, and explicit.	**Planning:** Based on our analysis, which needs are highest-leverage? What two or three mini-lessons or experiences could directly support these groups? **Monitoring:** Are the actions anchored in explicit instruction and success criteria? Do they build surface, deep, and transfer learning? **Evaluating:** How will we know these actions worked? What evidence will we collect before/after to track growth? **Acting:** Implement targeted mini-lessons/scaffolds and plan to revisit evidence in the next cycle.

This model redefines what it means to teach and learn in community. Students become co-learners and co-leaders, not passive recipients of instruction. In doing so, they strengthen their learner identities and develop the critical thinking, reflective inquiry, and collaboration skills essential to succeeding in dynamic, democratic societies. Learn more about how Impact Teams operationalize metacognitive clarity and learner agency in Chapter 9.

Consider these examples across disciplines enhanced through Impact Teams:

- **Visual Arts:** Students collaboratively define quality criteria for an art exhibition, regularly using Impact Team meetings to critique their works, refine their techniques, and align their creative expressions to meaningful community issues.
- **Science:** Lab groups function as Impact Teams, collectively analyzing experimental data to clarify scientific understanding, refining their hypotheses, and adapting their inquiry processes.
- **English Language Arts:** Students utilize Impact Team core formative practices during peer-conferencing sessions, systematically analyzing narrative drafts using co-created rubrics, clarifying storytelling strategies, and identifying shared next steps for deeper revision and reflection.

By introducing Impact Teams into collaborative practices, schools don't merely enhance academic outcomes—they nurture a thriving culture of continuous, metacognitive reflection and collective efficacy.

The Architecture Is Emotional

Clarity isn't purely cognitive; it thrives when intertwined with emotional clarity. Emotional safety, belonging, and self-awareness are foundational conditions for meaningful learning (Ambrose et al., 2010). Two frameworks anchor emotional clarity:

- **CASEL's SEL Competencies** include self-awareness, self-management, social awareness, relationship skills, and responsible decision-making. In Chapter 4, we elaborate on the reciprocal relationship between metacognition and SEL.
- **Learning Dispositions** include curiosity, resilience, flexibility, criticality, and self-efficacy.

When teachers routinely leverage these frameworks, they foster environments where students courageously engage, authentically reflect, and continuously transfer learning beyond classroom walls.

Emotional Safety Fuels Cognition

Emotionally safe classrooms quiet the brain's stress response, improving access to memory and reasoning centers like the hippocampus and prefrontal cortex (Hammond, 2015). Consider these examples across contexts:

- **Performing Arts:** Drama students build emotional clarity by openly reflecting on their feelings during improvisational exercises, developing resilience and adaptability while enhancing their self-awareness on stage.
- **Mathematics:** Learners apply responsible decision-making by collaboratively reflecting on moments of frustration during complex problem-solving, discussing strategies to manage stress, build perseverance, and enhance their mathematical self-efficacy.
- **Social Studies:** Students cultivate social awareness and empathy by exploring historical events through role-play scenarios, engaging deeply with diverse perspectives, and reflecting on how these emotional insights impact their critical understanding of history.
- **English Language Arts:** Literature circles foster emotional safety by encouraging students to share personal connections to stories, thereby nurturing curiosity, criticality, and relationship skills through genuine peer dialogue and reflection.

When metacognitive clarity and emotional clarity intertwine, students don't just navigate learning—they thrive within it. These interconnected frameworks transform classrooms into communities of courageous inquiry, empathetic dialogue, and authentic reflection. By intentionally cultivating trust, belonging, and shared ownership, educators empower students to continuously grow their understanding and agency, extending meaningful learning far beyond the classroom. In doing so, metacognitive clarity becomes more than a surface-level strategy; it evolves into a powerful, deeply humanizing approach to education. Refer to Chapter 4 for a deeper dive into how social-emotional learning, identity, and metacognition intersect to support whole-child development.

Download a copy of *Creating Conditions for Metacognition*, in the Learning Tools for Clarity of Purpose under the heading *Identity, Justice, and Belonging as Foundations* to reflect on how classrooms do or can impact students' psychological safety, identity, belonging, and inclusion.

Toward Transformative Possibility

Metacognitive clarity is an instructional practice foundational to transformative learning. Moreover, its effectiveness is grounded in neuroscientific evidence, as shared in our Neuroscience Notes throughout the text. It aligns deeply with learner identity, empowering students to actively shape their educational journeys with clarity of purpose, process, and ownership.

When clarity moves beyond surface-level understanding, it cultivates essential democratic capacities: critical reflection, collaborative responsibility, and justice-driven action. Students who are empowered to co-construct learning intentions, success criteria, and assessments within emotionally safe, culturally responsive communities become authentically engaged, empathetic, and resilient. In these vibrant learning spaces, students and educators not only pursue academic success but also share the goal of shaping a more just and equitable society.

Reflect and Act

Reflect

Take a moment to pause and look inward:

How does your own identity as a learner—shaped by your lived experiences, culture, and values—influence the way you engage with your students' learning?

Now reflect on your students:

How often do your students see themselves, their aspirations, identities, and community wisdom reflected in the learning process?

Now consider:

Where in your practice can clarity move from a teacher-delivered concept to a co-constructed, student-empowered experience?

Act

1. **Invite students to co-construct clarity**

    Partner to clarify not just learning goals, but in the purpose, process, and ownership of learning itself.

    - *Example:* Begin a new unit by discussing with students what they hope to learn and how they might demonstrate their understanding, then co-create the unit's success criteria together.

2. **Facilitate regular reflective dialogues**

    Honor students' cultural strengths, personal narratives, and evolving learner identities.

    - *Example:* Set aside time each week for small group discussions, where students share personal connections to the content or reflect on their growth as learners.

3. **Nurture emotional clarity**

    Embed practices that promote safety, belonging, and resilience as daily, shared responsibilities in the classroom.

    - *Example:* Use daily check-ins or community circles, where students can express how they're feeling and identify supports they need to thrive.

When we see metacognitive clarity as a profoundly democratic and inclusive practice, we move beyond compliance or performance. We invite learners into a shared space of inquiry, where voice, identity, and purpose fuel authentic engagement and collective transformation.

While supporting student learning, you are co-building a community where everyone grows together.

CHAPTER 2
THE HIDDEN ENGINE OF LEARNING

Democracy must be born every generation anew, and education is its midwife.
— **John Dewey, 1916**

Metacognition is often described simply as "thinking about thinking," but this modest phrase belies its transformative power. At its core, metacognition is a dynamic, intentional process—one in which learners of all ages actively plan, monitor, and evaluate their thinking to deepen understanding and promote growth. This chapter explores the rich, cyclical nature of metacognition and how it fosters self-regulation, agency, and resilience, not only in students but also in the adults who teach, lead, and collaborate in learning communities. When embraced collectively, metacognition becomes a powerful driver of change, fueling fiercely participatory classrooms, collaborative teams, and inclusive schools grounded in equity, shared leadership, and democratic values.

In democratic classrooms, learning is anything but passive; it's fiercely active and participatory. The metacognitive cycle equips students to navigate learning with purpose. It ensures that every voice counts, that every learner has influence, and reflection serves not merely personal gain but collective good.

The Metacognitive Cycle

We view the metacognitive cycle (see Figure 2.1) as a dynamic way of being—a mindset that supports growth, learning, and adaptation for *all* learners, across all roles and stages of life. Whether you're a student, a teacher, a leader, or any adult in the system, this cycle offers a flexible, recursive process that mirrors the realities of learning in an ever-changing world. It empowers individuals to reflect deeply, make intentional choices, and respond to challenges with clarity and resilience. Those who internalize the cycle approach learning with purpose, navigate complexity with agility, and take collective responsibility for the communities they serve. In fact, we often unknowingly run the Plan–Monitor–Evaluate cycle in the course of our daily lives—for example, when we plan or adjust a commute, budget for and engage in a home renovation project, or make mid-course corrections such as pivoting mid-lesson or mid-meeting in response to unforeseen situations or outcomes. When we inquire into these everyday routines and name the strategies used, we surface metacognitive expertise that's already there and sharpen it with purpose.

Figure 2.1: The Metacognitive Cycle

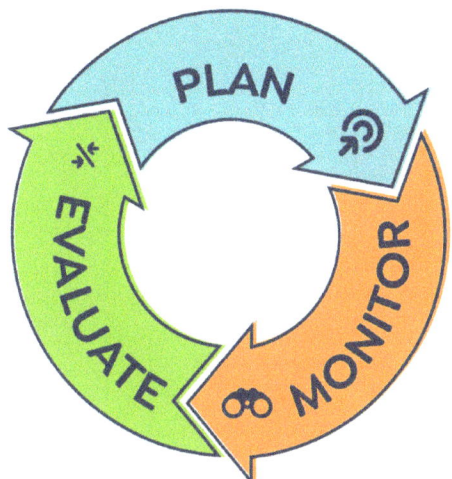

PLAN

- Set a clear goal
- Analyze a model
- Co-construct success criteria
- Choose strategies and tools
- Schedule checkpoints

MONITOR

- Check against success criteria
- Collect quick evidence
- Use self-talk or partner feedback
- Adjust strategies, time, or supports

EVALUATE

- Compare final work to success criteria/model
- Name what strategies/conditions worked and why
- Identify growth and needs
- Set next steps: revise, practice, or extend

The cycle revolves around three essential stages:

- **Plan**
  - Set goals
  - Determine strategies
  - Predict outcomes
  - Identify resources needed

- **Monitor**
  - Track progress toward goals
  - Adjust strategies if necessary
  - Check understanding and self-questioning
  - Recognize obstacles or confusion

- **Evaluate**
  - Reflect on performance
  - Assess the effectiveness of strategies
  - Consider what worked and what didn›t
  - Make adjustments for future tasks

Each stage thrives on powerful questions that guide learners' cognitive growth and help them contribute meaningfully to their communities.

Stage 1: Plan

Charting a Path With Purpose

Effective learning begins well before action is taken. In the Plan stage, students set clear intentions, anticipate obstacles, and choose strategies grounded in experience. It's about learners seeing beyond individual success, embracing their role in fostering an equitable, inclusive learning space.

Key Metacognitive Questions for Planning:

- What is my goal, and how does it serve the broader community?
- What knowledge or experience do I have that could help others?
- What are some strategies that I've used in the past that might apply here?
- What strategies can enhance both my understanding and collective learning?
- What potential obstacles could we encounter, and how can we tackle them fairly and compassionately?

- What would success look like for our learning community and me?
- Who can I lean on and learn from?

Planning doesn't merely set goals; it sparks proactive action. It empowers learners to become architects of their learning paths.

Stage 2: Monitor

Staying the Course, Adapting in Motion

Great learning involves continuous calibration. Monitoring means learners regularly check in with their understanding, adjust strategies, and regulate emotions amid challenges. It also prompts learners to consider their actions within the broader learning environment.

Key Metacognitive Questions for Monitoring:

- Am I progressing toward my goal and supporting my peers in reaching theirs?
- Should I adjust my approach to be more effective or inclusive?
- What am I noticing about what's working—and what's not—for myself and our group?
- How are my emotions and focus contributing to a supportive, equitable environment?
- Who can I support? Who can support me as I work through this?

Monitoring isn't merely about progress checks; it's about cultivating adaptability and resilience, nurturing a deep sense of agency and responsibility toward oneself and one's community.

Stage 3: Evaluate

Looking Back, Moving Forward

Reflection transforms learning experiences into profound insights. When learners reflect, they convert experiences into powerful revelations. Evaluation guides them to critically analyze outcomes, revisit chosen methods, and set ambitious yet achievable goals. In doing so, learners acknowledge their growth while recognizing the roles in promoting fairness, inclusion, and collective empowerment.

Key Metacognitive Questions for Evaluating:

- Did I meet my goal? Why or why not?
- How did my strategies impact my own learning and that of my peers?
- What could I do differently next time to enhance fairness, inclusivity, and collective understanding?
- What have I discovered about myself as both a learner and a democratic participant?

Evaluation reframes mistakes as valuable learning opportunities—emphasizing growth, continuous improvement, and collective advancement.

Making Sense of Knowledge Types Through Metacognition

When we sharpen our understanding of different types of knowledge, we are better equipped to engage in deep learning that goes well beyond simply acquiring and memorizing information; metacognition is the bridge to such understanding. By explicitly connecting declarative, procedural, and conceptual knowledge to metacognitive strategies, learners develop the capacity to independently manage, adapt, and extend their learning. Here's how these knowledge types (See Figure 2.2) and their metacognitive connections can be understood:

- **Declarative Knowledge (Knowing "What"):** Facts, definitions, and concepts

  - *Example:* Identifying moon phases by name (new moon, crescent, gibbous)
  - **Metacognitive Connection:** Students employ strategies such as self-questioning ("Do I recall the definition clearly and accurately?") to assess and strengthen their understanding and retention.

- **Procedural Knowledge (Knowing "How"):** Processes, skills, and actions

  - *Example:* Modeling moon phases using a Styrofoam ball and a lamp to simulate Earth, Moon, and Sun positions
  - **Metacognitive Connection:** Students use self-monitoring techniques to evaluate the effectiveness of their procedural steps ("Am I modeling this accurately? Do I need to adjust my approach?").

- **Conceptual Knowledge (Knowing "Why"):** Interrelationships and underlying principles connecting ideas

  - *Example:* Understanding why Moon phases occur due to Earth–Moon–Sun interactions
  - **Metacognitive Connection:** Students engage in deeper reflective practices such as concept mapping, analogies, or self-explanations ("How do these concepts interconnect? Can I clearly articulate why this phenomenon occurs?") to solidify their conceptual understanding.

Metacognition transforms these knowledge types from static information into dynamic learning processes. Learners don't simply memorize (declarative), execute tasks (procedural), or analyze relationships (conceptual); they actively engage through planning, monitoring, and evaluating each step. They self-question ("Do I understand this moon phase clearly?"), monitor progress ("Is this model accurately representing the phases of the Moon?"), and reflect critically ("How does this demonstrate the relationship between the Earth and the Moon?").

Figure 2.2: Types of Knowledge

Through metacognition, knowledge moves from surface-level memorization to deeper, transferable understanding, preparing students not just to recall or perform, but to apply what they know to novel situations creatively.

That's So Meta(cognitive):

Check out *That's So Meta(cognitive)* from the Smithsonian Science Education Center, which investigates how explicitly teaching students metacognitive strategies helps them become more effective learners, able to integrate knowledge rather than just memorize isolated science facts and definitions.

Metacognition Shapes Leaders, Learners, and Liberators

Metacognition, at its best, cultivates leaders capable of reshaping society. When students master the art of reflecting deeply on their thinking, they become empowered learners, democratic citizens, and active agents of liberation. The magic of the metacognitive cycle is its subtle strength. It builds critical capacities essential for thriving both personally and communally:

- **Self-Regulation:** Students learn to manage their attention, emotions, and actions, becoming active drivers of their education.
- **Agency:** Internalizing this cycle convinces learners they hold the power to shape their outcomes through strategic effort, adaptation, and advocacy for justice.
- **Resilience:** Challenges become integral parts of learning and opportunities to refine strategies, spurring continuous growth.
- **Democracy:** Metacognition fosters the democratic skills of self-awareness, critical thinking, collaboration, and communal responsibility.
- **Justice:** Reflective practice heightens awareness of fairness, amplifies voices, and positions learners as active changemakers in their communities.

Explicitly modeling and teaching the metacognitive cycle transforms learning. Students internalize these strategies, learning to master content and to shape democratic, equitable communities. In short, metacognition becomes a transformative force—shaping leaders, empowering learners, and inspiring committed liberators capable of envisioning and realizing more equitable and democratic societies.

Cognitive and Metacognitive Strategies: A Harmonious Partnership

The prefix *meta* denotes something self-referential. An example that will probably be familiar to tech-savvy readers is the term "metadata," which means data about data. As mentioned previously, a simple (albeit reductionist) definition of metacognition is "thinking about thinking." The distinction between cognitive and metacognitive strategies is essential. Cognitive strategies are the specific methods learners use to engage with content. For example, a social studies student needs to understand the concept of checks and balances in government. Cognitive strategies might include reading and re-reading portions of the textbook and underlining or highlighting relevant portions. In other words, they use such cognitive strategies to focus directly on completing the learning task at hand.

In contrast, students use metacognitive strategies to step back from the learning task to evaluate and direct the use of cognitive strategies. They will decide which cognitive strategy is appropriate, monitor its effectiveness, and adjust as needed. Let's assume that our social studies student has memorized the three branches of the United States government but still struggles to explain the powers and checks they exercise over one another. They might begin with self-questioning, such as, "What do I already know about the branches of government? What do I need to know?" They might then create a chart with separate columns for Branch, Powers, and Checks on other branches.

Neuroscience Insight: Reflection Builds Neural Flexibility

When students reflect on their thinking, they engage the dorsolateral prefrontal cortex—a region sometimes called the brain's "thinking coach" because it helps us pause, plan, and choose new strategies. Strengthening this area boosts students' ability to adjust their approach, stick with challenges, and grow into more independent, flexible learners (Zelazo & Lyons, 2012).

Supporting Neurodiverse Learners and Students With Learning Disabilities

Metacognition flourishes when every learner has an authentic way to access it. For students who are neurodiverse or who experience learning disabilities, equitable access means more than accommodations; it means recognizing and designing for the full range of how minds work. When educators adapt the metacognitive cycle and create multiple pathways for accessing and expressing metacognitive awareness, they affirm that all students can plan, monitor, and evaluate their thinking with purpose.

This begins by offering multiple entry points into reflection and strategy development. Some learners process ideas through movement, others through mapping or drawing, and others through dialogue or storytelling. A variety of tools, including journals, concept maps, audio recordings, and kinesthetic activities, invite students to refine their thinking in ways that feel natural and meaningful.

Metacognitive practice also takes distinct forms across neurotypes. A student with ADHD may benefit from frequent check-ins and external scaffolds to sustain focus. An autistic student may excel at detailed self-analysis but need guidance to shift strategies in new contexts. A student with dyslexia may rely more on listening and oral reasoning than on written text. In each case, metacognition helps the learner improve their relationship with and understanding of the content and strengthens a way of thinking they can use for the rest of their lives.

Explicit attention to executive functioning skills, such as working memory, attention, and cognitive flexibility, further strengthens this work. When learners understand how these processes affect their strategies, they gain clarity and confidence. A student who recognizes limits in working memory might create a checklist, while another may use audio notes to monitor comprehension. Such awareness normalizes difference and shifts classrooms from accommodation to genuine inclusion, affirming that every learner can engage fully in the metacognitive cycle.

Cognitive and metacognitive strategies work best in partnership. Cognitive strategies help learners engage directly with content, while metacognitive strategies provide the reflection and adjustment that make those efforts effective. When classrooms honor diverse ways of thinking and include explicit attention to executive functioning, every learner can participate fully in planning, monitoring, and evaluating. This harmony not only strengthens learning but also advances equity, inclusion, and democratic participation.

Infusing Metacognition

Metacognitive strategies align seamlessly with the three stages of the metacognitive cycle: plan, monitor, and evaluate. During the planning stage, strategies such as goalsetting, previewing, and activating prior knowledge help learners prepare intentionally for their tasks. Using explicit instruction, educators model "planning" through think-alouds where they explain and model—articulating how they identify goals and select appropriate approaches. In the monitoring stage, strategies such as questioning, summarizing, and visualizing enable learners to actively track and adjust their comprehension in real time; teachers gradually release responsibility by first demonstrating these strategies explicitly, then guiding practice through scaffolding and feedback. Finally, in the evaluation stage, learners reflect critically on their performance and learning process, employing strategies like self-assessment, analyzing effectiveness, and adjusting future approaches. Through explicit modeling and guided reflection, educators help students internalize and independently apply these strategies, enhancing their overall metacognitive clarity and learning effectiveness.

For practical application, two resources in the Learning Tools for Clarity of Process under the heading *Navigating the Metacognitive Cycle* offer guidance: *A Flow for Teaching Metacognitive Strategies Effectively* provides a step-by-step process for introducing and modeling strategies, while the *Developmental Progression for Metacognitive Clarity* offers a K–12 roadmap for introducing, scaffolding, and deepening them. Together, they provide both the "how" and the "when/what" for each stage of learner growth.

Bringing It All Together: From Tasks to Transformation

By now, it should be clear that continued use of the metacognitive cycle elevates students from passive and compliant recipients of instruction into active architects of their educational journey and future leaders of their communities. The following is an example of the transformative power of metacognitive clarity.

- **Plan:** Before beginning an inquiry into local water quality disparities affecting different neighborhoods, students collaboratively set intentional goals anchored in environmental justice. They ask themselves and each other: *What inequities exist in our community's access to clean water? Who is most affected and why? How can our investigation and actions promote fairness and sustainability for everyone?* By grounding their goals in equity, students plan with clear intention, preparing strategies to ensure inclusive participation.

- **Monitor:** As students gather water samples, analyze contamination data, and research historical and social contexts, they remain attentive to both their scientific inquiry and their collective progress toward justice-oriented outcomes. They reflect continuously: *Are our methods equitable? Are we listening respectfully to one another? Are we listening respectfully to community perspectives? Have we adequately included data that represents marginalized voices?* Adjustments are made not just to enhance scientific accuracy but to sustain a responsive, inclusive process.

- **Evaluate:** At the close of their inquiry, students engage in deep, collective reflection about the impacts of their work. They explore questions such as: *Did our investigation uplift community voices traditionally marginalized? How effectively did our proposed solutions address both scientific findings and systemic injustices? What steps can we take together next to further support environmental justice in our community?* Their evaluation transcends personal performance, guiding them toward collective growth, systemic impact, and continuous improvement.

When students internalize this metacognitive cycle through experiences rooted in the example that centers on environmental justice, learning becomes more than a checklist—it becomes a call to leadership. They move from compliance to active contribution, transforming themselves into strategic, reflective agents of positive change.

Reflect and Act

Reflect

- How often do students explicitly plan, monitor, and evaluate their learning with a focus on community impact?
- Where in your practice could students strengthen their democratic and reflective habits?

Act

Commit to one deliberate shift:

1. **Model goal setting with community purpose**
   - Explicitly demonstrate how to set goals that serve both individual learning and collective well-being.

2. **Build routines for monitoring progress together**
   - Encourage students to routinely check not only their own progress but also how they are supporting peers and contributing to group success.

3. **Elevate evaluation as a communal practice**
   - Facilitate evaluations that emphasize collective improvement, inclusivity, and democratic reflection.

Fostering reflective, democratic engagement transforms classrooms into spaces where students are not just learners, but community leaders. By embedding the metacognitive cycle into daily practice, you move beyond compliance to cultivate agency, responsibility, and shared leadership.

CHAPTER 3

THE CONDITIONS THAT LIBERATE THINKING

Education either functions as an instrument to bring about conformity or freedom.
— Paulo Freire

Metacognition doesn't emerge from thin air; it thrives or withers based on the conditions we create in our classrooms and schools. This chapter explores three essential conditions—psychological safety, identity affirmation, and belonging—that collectively fuel metacognitive equity, which, in its purest form, means that *all* students have access to metacognitive clarity. We also address some of the more common hidden barriers to achieving and sustaining metacognitive clarity, as well as some ways in which we can counteract them.

Psychological Safety: The Crucible of Courageous Thinking

When Google conducted a long-term study of why some of its teams are more effective than others, its researchers identified psychological safety as the single most important influence on high-performing teams. Think about your own workplace and ask yourself the following: Can I speak openly, fail publicly, and question bravely without fear of ridicule or judgment? If your answer is an unequivocal "yes," you are fortunate enough to have experienced psychological safety! Similarly, classrooms that nurture psychological safety are spaces that liberate students from the crushing burdens of fear and shame. Such classrooms are natural incubators for authentic metacognition.

When learners feel safe enough to say, "I don't understand yet," or "Here's where I'm stuck," they start planning, monitoring, and evaluating honestly. Psychological safety transforms the fear of mistakes into opportunities for deep learning.

To cultivate psychological safety:

- Normalize struggles as vital parts of learning.
- Meet confusion with curiosity rather than frustration.
- Model vulnerability: "Today, I stumbled here—this is how I adapted."
- Establish norms that protect risk-taking and reflective honesty.

Safety protects and empowers. It turns classrooms into spaces where learners authentically own their thinking.

Identity Affirmation: The Power of Story

Metacognition isn't abstract; it's intensely personal. It's shaped by the stories learners tell themselves about who they are as thinkers. In Chapter 1, we discussed the relationship between learner identity and one's capacity for metacognition. However, one's learner identity is informed by intersecting facets of identity that are equally important. For thinking to truly thrive, students must see their identities—cultural, linguistic, and experiential—as strengths, not deficits.

Seminal research from Moll et al. (1992), Ladson-Billings (1995), and more recent studies (Dee & Penner, 2017; Paris & Alim, 2017) highlight that when students are encouraged to engage and draw from their cultural assets, they perform better academically and socially than peers who are not given those opportunities. When learners' narratives and languages are woven into classroom practices, they connect more deeply with their learning process.

Identity and Learning Are Neurologically Linked

When students feel heard and seen, their brains activate the default mode network—a system that helps us reflect on ourselves, connect to our values, and make meaning of new information. This strengthens motivation, emotional engagement, and learning (Marcus et al., 2020). Without affirmation, thinking becomes compliance rather than empowerment. But when identity is celebrated, students don't just engage with content; they claim ownership of their learning journey.

To affirm learner identities:

- Integrate students' cultural knowledge into learning tasks.
- Celebrate multilingual practices as academic strengths.
- Highlight diverse intellectual traditions and thinkers.
- Offer multiple pathways for planning, reflection, and sharing.
- Invite students to author their own learning stories.

Identity affirmation, among other things, is simply the right thing to do. It not only promotes the development of metacognitive skills but also fuels cultural and linguistic sustainability. Effective educators recognize that affirming identities also means affirming family stories, values, and cultural assets. Family engagement deepens this affirmation, providing authentic, culturally relevant connections between home and school. To explore how powerful family–school partnerships foster identity affirmation and metacognitive equity, refer to Chapter 10: "Amplifying Metacognitive Clarity Through Family–School Partnerships."

Belonging: Why Community Is the Root of Great Thinking

The meaning of "belonging" might seem elusive, but its absence is painfully obvious. Without it, learners retreat, withholding insights that could transform their learning community. Belonging is more than feeling welcomed—it's feeling valued.

Emotional Safety Fuels Cognition

Belonging lowers emotional threat, freeing up the hippocampus and prefrontal cortex for deeper learning. The hippocampus helps us store and recall new information, while the prefrontal cortex supports focus, planning, and decision-making—key functions that thrive when students feel safe and valued (Immordino-Yang, 2016). When students sense, "I matter here," they engage courageously in reflection, risk-taking, and collaborative inquiry. They lean into uncertainty, trusting their community will support rather than judge their evolving thoughts. Belonging anchors students, enabling them to stretch beyond their comfort zones.

Strategies to cultivate belonging:

- Frame learning as a shared mission: "Our collective growth depends on every voice."
- Use collaborative routines that showcase diverse insights.
- Co-create classroom norms, empowering student voices.
- Celebrate effort, growth, and thoughtful risk-taking.
- Recognize and validate emotional journeys in learning.

Belonging shifts metacognition from a solitary endeavor to a communal experience. It democratizes the learning process, making each student a vital contributor.

The Metacognitive Equity Framework

The three conditions explored above—psychological safety, identity affirmation, and belonging—are not isolated practices. Together, they create the environment in which metacognitive equity becomes possible by ensuring that every learner has genuine access to metacognitive clarity. When students feel safe, seen, and connected, they gain the freedom to think bravely, reflect honestly, and act with growing agency.

Figure 3.1 illustrates this relationship. When classrooms honor individual identities and cultivate true belonging, they generate the psychological safety required for courageous thinking. In this crucible, students are freed from fear, affirmed in who they are, and empowered to engage fully in metacognition.

Figure 3.1: Metacognitive Equity

Teaching the Craft of Metacognition: From Skill to Agency

Metacognition is a learned skill. It must be explicitly taught, modeled, and practiced. Harvard's Project Zero underscores that Visible Thinking routines—structured activities that sharpen students' metacognitive skills—significantly improve critical thinking and reflection.[1] Yet despite the evidence that supports teaching metacognitive skills, all too often this powerful practice is left to chance or privilege.

Teaching metacognition is an act of justice. It equips every learner, not just a privileged few, to strategize, adapt, and advocate for their learning needs. Historically, explicit metacognitive instruction has often been reserved for gifted education programs or elite college-preparatory institutions, unintentionally reinforcing educational inequities. By making these skills universally accessible, we empower students by dismantling barriers and ensuring that every learner has the tools to thrive academically and beyond. Explicitly cultivating metacognitive practices transforms classrooms from passive information exchanges into vibrant democracies of thought.

Core practices for teaching metacognition:

- Think aloud routinely: "I'm planning my next step because . . ."; "I'm adjusting because . . ."
- Scaffold reflection using structured sentence starters.

  - "This changes the way I understand because . . ."
  - "I'm beginning to see a bigger idea about . . ."
  - "I wonder how this connects to _____. This is something I didn't expect."
  - "I'm struggling to understand _____, and that tells me . . ."
  - "This moment is important because it reveals . . ."

- Integrate regular pauses in instruction dedicated to planning, monitoring, and evaluating.
- Celebrate strategic thinking, adaptation, and persistence—not just correctness.
- Create spaces where thinking, strategies, and insights are publicly shared.

By teaching metacognition explicitly, educators transform students into strategic thinkers capable of shaping their own learning narratives, while immersion in discourse strengthens questioning, reasoning, and collaborative meaning-making.

See the *Process* section of the appendices for step-by-step guidance on explicit metacognition instruction including modeling, guided practice, and scaffolds that turn safety, affirmation, and belonging into lived practices of metacognitive equity.

---

1. Harvard Project Zero, founded in 1967 by philosopher Nelson Goodman at the Harvard Graduate School of Education, is an influential research center dedicated to understanding learning processes, creativity, critical thinking, and human potential. Project Zero explores educational practices that foster deep understanding, inquiry, and collaborative thinking, developing frameworks such as Visible Thinking, Teaching for Understanding, and Making Learning Visible. Its work is characterized by an emphasis on learner agency, reflective thinking, and interdisciplinary connections (Ritchhart et al., 2011).

Dismantling Hidden Barriers to Metacognitive Access

Barriers to metacognitive equity often hide in plain sight—in curriculum, language, and implicit expectations set by educators and society at large. Carol Dweck's groundbreaking research on growth and fixed mindsets reveals how subtle yet powerful messages about intelligence can profoundly shape students' self-beliefs (2008). Simply stated, those with fixed mindsets (and this can include both students and teachers) believe that intelligence and ability are "hardwired," whereas those with growth mindsets believe that these qualities can be developed with time and effort. Students who internalize deficit beliefs about their capabilities—illustrated by fixed statements like, "I'm just not good at math"—perceive their abilities as static and unchangeable. Consequently, rather than engaging in metacognitive strategies that will enhance their self-efficacy and, ultimately, further their progress in math, they are held back by deficit beliefs such as, "Why bother? It's just the way I am." While we affirm that an understanding of mindsets can be useful to both teachers and students, it comes with a cautionary note. Educator Rick Wormeli (2018) warns that an overemphasis on growth mindset alone[2] risks perpetuating deficit thinking. Such frameworks can unintentionally reinforce stereotypes, blaming marginalized students rather than addressing structural inequities, systemic biases, and unjust educational conditions that profoundly affect their ability to learn and grow.

Another barrier related to a fixed mindset is a narrow definition of intelligence. The misuse of IQ testing for "sorting purposes" fueled the eugenics movement. Later, the curriculum was narrowed to privilege reading and math at the expense of other subjects. Students were fed a bland diet of worksheets and low-rigor tasks in the name of "remediation." At the same time, schools often disregarded students' cultural assets and ways of knowing. These misguided assumptions about what it means to be "smart" have worked against metacognitive access, especially for our most underserved students.

Finally, pressure to cover what some have called a "mile-wide and inch-deep" curriculum has resulted in rushed instructional environments that deny students reflective opportunities. In an effort to check off or "cover" numerous standards, educators often sacrifice depth, leading to superficial understanding and limiting students' opportunities to engage thoughtfully with their own learning processes. This hurried pace leaves little room for students to develop the reflective habits essential to metacognitive growth. It disproportionately disadvantages scores of learners who already face systemic obstacles, thus perpetuating educational inequities.

Steps to dismantle barriers:

- Audit curricula for implicit bias and rigid definitions of "good thinking."
- Intentionally carve out space for reflection and dialogue in every lesson.
- Reframe all learners as evolving strategic thinkers, avoiding binary labels like "smart" or "struggling."
- Validate diverse cultural frameworks for thinking and reasoning.

---

2. Wormeli argues that the same holds true for a related concept, "grit" (Duckworth, 2016), which refers to one's ability to persevere—even when confronted by challenges and setbacks. When the grit concept is misapplied in a manner that supports deficit thinking (e.g., "those kids will never succeed: they just don't have grit"), the consequences are harmful.

Removing these barriers doesn't merely enhance individual learning—it reshapes classrooms into equitable communities of strategic thinkers.

From Better Thinking to Democratic Action

The true power of metacognition isn't only in thinking better—it's in acting democratically. When students regularly practice metacognition, they rehearse civic actions of self-governance, collaborative responsibility, and active citizenship. In each reflective pause, learners not only refine their academic strategies but deepen their democratic commitments.

Creating the conditions for metacognitive equity doesn't merely produce better students; it shapes thoughtful citizens. Psychological safety, identity affirmation, belonging, and barrier removal aren't just educational goals—they are democratic imperatives.

In the next chapter, we'll examine how fostering dispositions like curiosity, resilience, and criticality sustains democratic thinking and enriches lifelong learning.

Reflect and Act

Metacognitive equity is not a luxury reserved for some students. Instead, think of it as a daily, democratic practice that benefits all students. Use the prompts below to pause, reflect, and take deliberate action in your classroom or leadership practice.

Psychological Safety: Laying the Groundwork

- Do I model vulnerability and normalize mistake-making?
- How do I respond when students say, *"I don't understand yet."*?
- What routines protect intellectual risk-taking and honest reflection?

Identity Affirmation: Honoring Every Story

- Whose cultural, linguistic, and experiential identities are visible in learning?
- How do I affirm multilingualism and diverse traditions as strengths?
- In what ways do I invite students to author and share their learning stories?

Belonging: Building Communities of Courageous Thinking

- Do all students know their voices matter here?
- How do we co-create norms and routines that honor every perspective?
- How do I recognize and support students' emotional journeys in learning?

Dismantling Hidden Barriers

- Who hesitates to speak or share, and why?
- What hidden expectations or biases might be limiting access to deeper thinking?
- What one barrier will I disrupt this week?

Action Steps
Choose one shift this week to move reflection into practice:

- Embed a daily reflective pause that normalizes struggle and celebrates strategy.
- Affirm identity through texts, tasks, or student storytelling.
- Revisit class norms with students to strengthen safety and belonging.
- Audit one lesson for bias or narrow definitions of "smartness" and redesign it.

Each intentional act, whether protecting risk-taking, affirming identity, cultivating belonging, or dismantling barriers, moves us closer to liberating thinking and sustaining democracy through metacognition.

CHAPTER 4

EDUCATING THE WHOLE LEARNER: INTEGRATING HEART, MIND, AND COMMUNITY

The whole is greater than the sum of its parts.
— **Aristotle**

Transformative learning engages the whole person, connecting the heart, mind, and body. It honors emotions, cultivates meaningful relationships, and recognizes the intricate ways every aspect of our being is interconnected. Holistic learning embraces this interconnectedness, emphasizing that each learner's academic growth is deeply tied to their emotional well-being, social connections, and cognitive agility. It acknowledges that authentic learning arises not from isolated parts but from nurturing and integrating all facets of an individual's experience.

To bring this vision to life in daily practice, educators need structures that reduce barriers and expand opportunities. Universal Design for Learning (UDL) offers such a framework by embedding flexibility and accessibility at the core of instruction. By providing multiple pathways for engagement, representation, and expression, UDL ensures that each learner can connect their heart, mind, and community in meaningful ways. Far from being an add-on, UDL is the design principle that makes holistic learning practical, inclusive, and sustainable.

Metacognitive clarity emerges naturally within this holistic vision. It's about helping students understand not just what they learn but how they think, feel, and relate to others. Drawing from visionary educators like Paulo Freire (1970), who saw education as a pathway to freedom and personal empowerment; bell hooks (1994), who championed education that integrates emotional, intellectual, and communal growth; and Gloria Ladson-Billings (1995), who advanced culturally relevant pedagogy to affirm students' identities while fostering academic excellence and critical consciousness, holistic education becomes genuinely transformative. Through metacognitive practices, learners develop a powerful awareness of their thinking patterns, emotions, and behaviors, enhancing their ability to navigate life's complexities with intention and empathy.

When classrooms fully embrace this enriched, purpose-driven approach, they become spaces where students build resilience, foster empathy, and actively engage in their communities. Education goes deeper than test scores; it's about developing people who can make a difference in the lives of others and their communities. By intentionally integrating Transformative Social-Emotional Learning (tSEL) with metacognitive strategies, educators inspire their students (CASEL, 2020). They empower learners to become reflective, proactive leaders, prepared to create a more equitable, just, and collectively flourishing society.

Family engagement plays a crucial role in supporting whole child education and tSEL by creating consistent, reinforcing environments that extend learning beyond school walls. When families are actively involved, children experience coherent messages about emotional regulation, relationship building, and character development across all their primary environments.

Transformative SEL goes beyond basic skill-building to help children develop authentic self-awareness, empathy, and social consciousness. Family engagement amplifies this deeper work by providing opportunities for children to practice emotional skills in real-world contexts with their most important relationships. Parents and caregivers can reinforce SEL concepts through family discussions, modeling emotional regulation during conflicts, and creating home environments that value emotional intelligence alongside academic achievement. See Chapter 10 for detailed strategies on leveraging family engagement for holistic learning, metacognition, and community impact.

Refer to the online appendices for extended tools, sample protocols, and additional resources connected to this chapter. These materials are designed to help you translate the big ideas of Chapter 4, and the rest of the book, into concrete practice.

The Transformative SEL Imperative

Transformative Social-Emotional Learning (tSEL) expands beyond traditional SEL frameworks by explicitly focusing on equity, justice, and community engagement (CASEL, 2020). Jagers, Rivas-Drake, and Williams (2019) emphasize that tSEL fosters critical self-reflection, prioritizes collective well-being, and prepares students to actively engage in meaningful change within their communities. According to the Collaborative for Academic, Social, and Emotional Learning (CASEL), the organization that first introduced the term social and emotional learning (SEL) over three decades ago, Transformative SEL (tSEL) involves establishing strong, respectful, and enduring relationships among young people and adults to support co-learning. It encourages critical analysis of both individual and contextual factors that perpetuate inequities and promotes collaborative solutions aimed at enhancing personal, community, and societal well-being (CASEL, n.d.). The CASEL tSEL framework represents a deeper, equity-centered extension of traditional SEL approaches.

Transformative SEL deeply aligns with CASEL's five core SEL competencies—self-awareness, self-management, social awareness, relationship skills, and responsible decision-making—by placing these competencies within a broader context of social justice and civic responsibility (CASEL, 2020). As Dena Simmons (2021) underscores, "SEL that fails to address our sociopolitical reality and combat racial and social injustice will not prepare our young people for the world they will inherit—one fraught with hate, misunderstanding, and bigotry." Integrating tSEL into learning experiences equips learners to critically engage with and meaningfully transform the world around them.

The three following categories, Critical Self-Reflection, Collective Well-Being, and Community Engagement and Action, are drawn from the CASEL Transformative SEL (tSEL) framework.

- **Critical Self-Reflection (Self-Awareness):**

  - *Classroom Example:* Students engage in regular journaling activities reflecting on personal identity, biases, and strengths. Through guided discussions, students share insights about their identities and learn about cultural humility, fostering deeper self-awareness and understanding.

- **Collective Well-Being (Social Awareness and Relationship Skills):**

  - *Classroom Example:* Students participate in cooperative projects, such as community-based problem-solving initiatives addressing local social issues. Through these projects, students practice empathy, build strong interpersonal skills, and strengthen their sense of collective responsibility.

- **Community Engagement and Action (Responsible Decision-Making):**

  - *Classroom Example:* Students collaboratively plan and implement service-learning projects addressing local environmental justice issues. They make collective decisions about project goals and strategies, and they evaluate impacts; this enhances responsible decision-making and reinforces their roles as active community members.

Transformative SEL instruction moves beyond simply teaching students to manage emotions and relationships by challenging them to engage thoughtfully, critically, and compassionately with their peers, communities, and the wider world. By centering critical self-reflection, collective well-being, and meaningful community action, we equip our students to become catalysts for positive social change. This is the transformative potential of education: nurturing learners with the awareness and motivation to actively question, collaborate, and advocate for equity and justice, embodying SEL as both a personal compass and a collective call to action.

Transformative SEL Introduction:

Chapter 3 highlights the conditions that liberate thinking—psychological safety, equity of voice, and shared inquiry. To see how these ideas come alive in the context of tSEL, refer to the overview video of Oregon's Transformative Social and Emotional Learning Framework. This narrated presentation illustrates how belonging, identity, and agency can be woven into daily instruction and scaled across schools and communities.

Integrating Executive Functioning, Self-Regulation, and SEL

In education, we often compartmentalize student growth, placing intellect in one corner, emotions in another, and behavior somewhere else—as though each operates independently. But when we look more closely, we see beyond compartments and begin to discern profound interconnectedness between academic achievement and emotions.

Similarly, executive functioning, self-regulation, and social-emotional learning aren't individual instruments performing separately; they form an integrated symphony. Executive functioning acts like the conductor, directing attention, organizing plans, and managing tasks. Self-regulation mirrors the musicians' tuning their instruments, adapting dynamically to changes in tempo and rhythm. Social-emotional learning represents the harmony that arises when musicians attentively listen and respond, balancing their contributions to create cohesive, resonant music. Each skill strengthens the next, creating a powerful combination of individual and social strengths. Metacognition—the ability to step back, reflect, and fine-tune the entire performance—deepens this synergy, enhancing the ensemble's overall performance.

Executive Skills Grow With Intentional Practice

Routines that strengthen planning, time management, and reflection activate the prefrontal cortex, the brain's command center for self-regulation. Just like physical muscles, these brain networks grow stronger with use—helping students become more organized, adaptable, and goal-driven over time (Diamond, 2013). This metaphorical symphony underscores how these elements are intricately connected, creating a continuous, reinforcing cycle of growth. Just as a conductor guides musicians to harmonize their instruments, a student's ability to plan and focus shapes their emotional responses, influencing their interactions and decisions.

Culturally responsive and sustaining practices acknowledge similar interconnectedness between body, mind, and spirit. Indigenous wisdom traditions, for instance, embrace a holistic understanding of individuals whose physical, emotional, intellectual, and spiritual dimensions are deeply entwined and inherently connected to family, community, and the land. In contrast to compartmentalized, Eurocentric educational systems, such integrated worldviews celebrate unity, interdependence, and harmony in relationships. By embracing these meaningful connections, educators empower themselves to intentionally nurture students' comprehensive growth, cultivating development precisely at the points where these vital dimensions intersect and thrive.

Figure 4.1 visually captures the interconnectedness among executive functioning, self-regulation, and social-emotional learning, illustrating how each supports and enriches the others, building a robust foundation for comprehensive learning development.

Figure 4.1: Holistic Learner Development

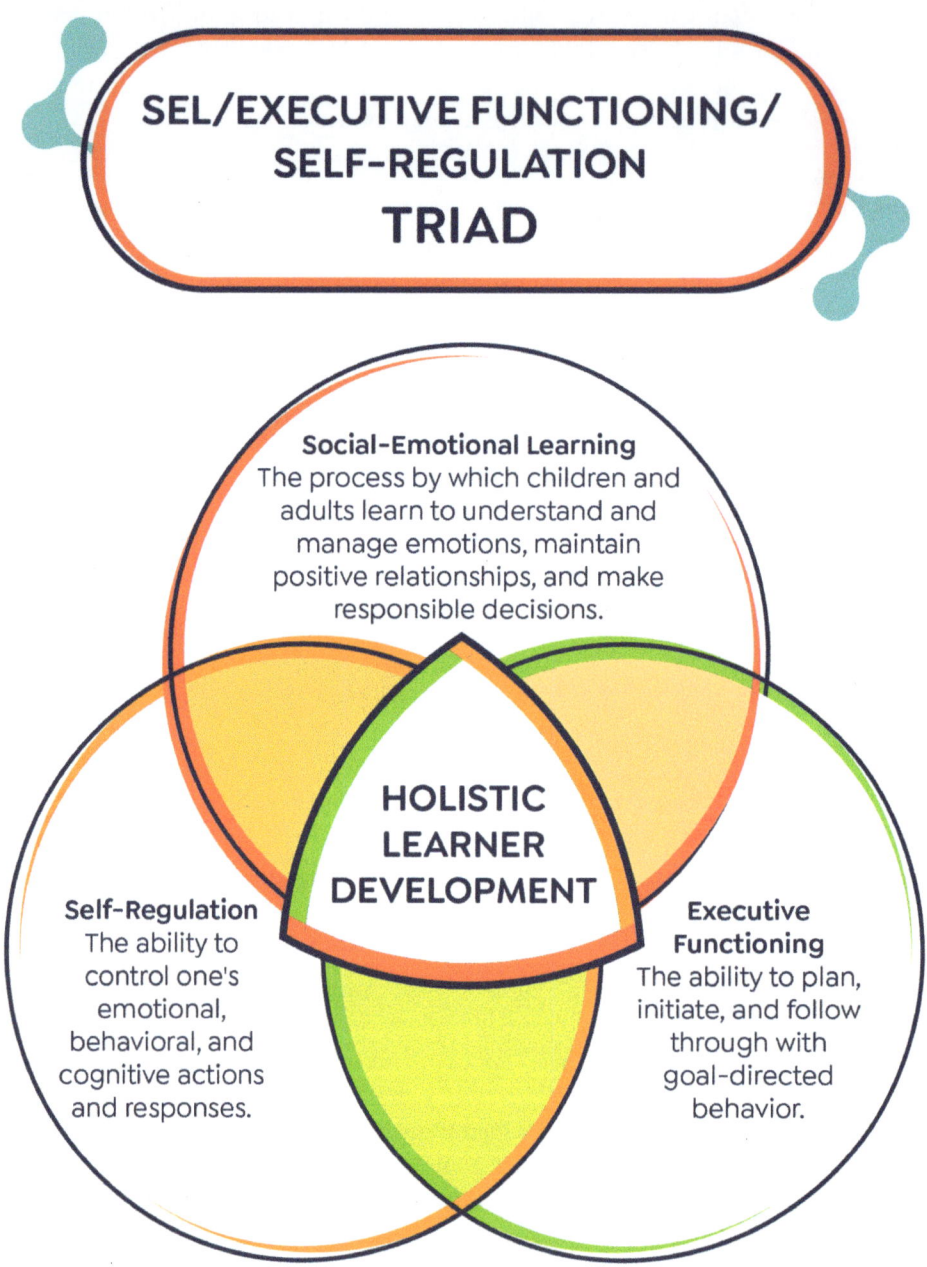

- **Executive Functioning:** This refers to the ability to plan, initiate, and execute goal-directed behaviors. It encompasses critical cognitive skills such as impulse control, emotional control, flexibility, working memory, self-monitoring, planning, prioritizing, task initiation, and organization. Strong executive functioning facilitates effective self-regulation and provides a foundational base for successful social-emotional learning.

- **Self-Regulation:** Defined as the ability to control one's emotional, behavioral, and cognitive actions and responses, self-regulation operates primarily as a stress-response system. It shares competencies with SEL, notably self-awareness, self-management, and social awareness. When self-regulation is weak, students may experience aggression, inattentiveness, hyperactivity, and reduced academic performance.

- **Social-Emotional Learning:** SEL encompasses the processes by which students and adults learn to understand and manage emotions, maintain positive relationships, and make responsible decisions. It consists of five interrelated competencies as identified by CASEL: self-awareness, self-management, social awareness, relationship skills, and responsible decision-making. Effective SEL is deeply associated with executive functioning, as the cognitive skills of executive functioning aid in the ability to delay gratification, manage conflicts, and engage fully in classroom learning.

SEL, Self-Regulation, and Executive Functioning: The Synergy

A holistic learning framework emphasizes that meaningful learner growth doesn't emerge from isolated skills or competencies but from their dynamic interconnectedness. Social-emotional learning, self-regulation, and executive functioning represent precisely such an interconnected system. Viewed holistically, these skills reinforce and enhance one another, enabling students to navigate complex academic and social environments more effectively. When learners master this integrative skillset, they become resilient problem-solvers, build deeper interpersonal connections, and experience stronger academic outcomes and personal well-being.

Key benefits and examples include:

- **Improved Emotional Resilience**
  Students recognize emotional triggers and practice emotional self-awareness (CASEL, 2020); respond calmly under stress through effective emotional regulation (Blair & Diamond, 2008); and strategically adapt responses to setbacks, leveraging cognitive flexibility inherent in executive functioning (Zelazo & Carlson, 2012).

- **Effective Conflict Resolution**
  Learners can empathize and understand diverse perspectives, enhancing social awareness (CASEL, 2020); manage impulsive reactions by employing self-control strategies (Duckworth & Carlson, 2013); and flexibly identify and negotiate collaborative solutions to disagreements, activating executive function skills like planning and adaptability (Diamond, 2013).

- **Enhanced Academic Performance**
  Students set clear, achievable learning goals and prioritize effectively through executive functioning skills such as working memory, planning, and self-monitoring (Best et al., 2011); maintain focus, attention, and regulate frustration during challenging learning tasks via self-regulation (McClelland & Cameron, 2012); and build self-confidence through SEL-driven reflective practices on goals and achievements (Durlak et al., 2011).

- **Stronger Interpersonal Relationships**
  Learners articulate their emotions clearly and demonstrate effective communication through SEL competencies, such as relationship skills (CASEL, 2020); exercise patience and impulse control when interacting with peers through behavioral self-regulation (Baumeister & Vohs, 2011); and strategically navigate social interactions with planning and adaptability—key executive function skills (Diamond, 2013).

- **Greater Self-Efficacy and Autonomy**
  Students independently organize study schedules and effectively prioritize tasks utilizing executive functioning skills like task initiation and time management (Meltzer, 2010); regulate motivation and sustain perseverance in challenging academic tasks through self-regulation strategies (Zimmerman, 2002); and enhance self-awareness and emotional reflection to foster self-efficacy through SEL competencies (Bandura, 1997; CASEL, 2020).

By actively cultivating this integrated set of skills, students become resilient, empathetic, and capable individuals, empowered to succeed both academically and personally.

Sown to Grow Demo and Overview:

This video shows how structured reflection and sharing strengthen SEL by fostering empathy, belonging, and voice. Sown to Grow makes this visible and practical, helping students connect heart, mind, and community.

Metacognition and SEL: A Reciprocal Relationship

Metacognition, the awareness and regulation of one's cognitive processes, complements SEL naturally. SEL provides the emotional foundation necessary for effective metacognition by nurturing self-awareness and emotional clarity, enabling learners to understand their emotional and cognitive processes deeply. Conversely, metacognition reinforces SEL by teaching students how to plan, monitor, and reflect on their emotional and social strategies, creating an integrated approach that promotes holistic growth.

Here are six practical examples across K–12 content areas and personal life, demonstrating the reciprocal relationship between metacognition and SEL:

1. **Elementary Mathematics (Content):**
   After struggling with a math word problem, a third-grader pauses and thinks, "I'm feeling frustrated. I'll take three deep breaths and then reread the problem slowly, step-by-step."

2. **Middle School Science (Content):**
   During a science experiment that isn't working as planned, a student recognizes anxiety building. They tell themselves, "It's okay to make mistakes. What can I adjust right now, and what can I ask my lab partner to help me clarify?"

3. **High School Literature (Content):**
   While reading a complex novel, a student realizes they're distracted and unable to en-

gage emotionally with the text. They stop to reflect: "Why am I feeling disconnected? Maybe I need to slow down and think about how the character's situation relates to my experiences."

4. **Peer Conflict (Personal Life):**
   Two friends argue at recess. One student, reflecting metacognitively, acknowledges internally: "I'm upset right now, but before I respond, I'll pause to think about why my friend might also feel hurt. I'll choose my words carefully to repair our friendship."

5. **Family Responsibilities (Personal Life):**
   A teenager feeling overwhelmed by chores at home recognizes their stress and uses self-talk: "I feel tense because I have so many responsibilities. I'll create a quick checklist and prioritize tasks to manage my time better and reduce stress."

6. **Preparing for a Performance (Personal Life):**
   A middle-school student experiences stage fright before a music recital. They acknowledge their nerves, calmly reminding themselves: "These feelings are normal. I've practiced and prepared. I'll visualize my success to build confidence."

These examples illustrate how students can use metacognition and SEL strategies together to effectively manage their academic challenges and personal life situations, fostering emotional resilience and cognitive growth.

Neuroscience Insights: Connecting Heart and Mind

Modern neuroscience underscores that emotional regulation, executive functioning, and metacognition share neural pathways, primarily within the prefrontal cortex. Research highlights that practices such as mindfulness, reflective journaling, and intentional emotional check-ins strengthen these neural connections, enhancing both emotional resilience and cognitive flexibility.

Specifically, SEL interventions activate neural regions associated with emotional regulation (amygdala and prefrontal cortex), executive functioning (prefrontal cortex), and metacognitive reflection (medial prefrontal cortex). By intentionally fostering these interconnected neural processes, educators not only support academic learning but also cultivate resilient, emotionally intelligent students who can navigate life's complexities.

Classroom Practices for Holistic Learning

Educators can embed Transformative SEL through deliberate classroom practices:

- **Reflective Practices:** Regular journaling, reflective dialogue, and mindfulness exercises encourage students to connect deeply with their emotional states, their bodies, and their thought processes.

   Grades K–2:
   - How are you feeling right now? Can you show me with your face or body?
   - What made you feel happy, sad, or excited today?

- Can you draw a picture that shows your feelings?

Grades 3–5:
- What emotions did you notice during today's activity? How did you manage them?
- How did your feelings affect your behavior today?
- What was one thing you learned about yourself through our mindfulness time?

Grades 6–8:
- What feelings came up during our reflection? What thoughts influenced these emotions?
- How does reflecting regularly help you handle stress or conflicts?
- What strategies did you use today to manage your emotions and thoughts?

Grades 9–12:
- How did today's mindfulness practice deepen your understanding of your emotional state?
- What recurring emotions or thoughts do you notice in your reflections?
- How do regular reflective practices help you connect more authentically with yourself and others?

Clarity Frees Brainpower

When students experience predictable routines, like check-ins, goal setting, or reflection, they use less mental energy figuring out what to do and more energy connecting with the learning. Clear structures reduce cognitive overload, making room for focus, memory, and engagement (Sweller et al., 2011).

- **Goal Setting and Monitoring:** Explicit instruction in goal-setting strategies, coupled with regular self-assessment and peer reflection, empowers students to practice executive functioning and self-regulation skills routinely.

Grades K–2:
- What is one thing you want to learn or do today?
- How can you tell if you're getting better at something?
- Who can help you reach your goals?

Grades 3–5:
- What goals did you set for yourself today or this week?
- How did you track your progress toward your goals?
- What did you do if you faced a challenge while working on your goals?

Grades 6–8:
- What specific strategies did you use to achieve your goal?
- How does goal setting help you stay focused and motivated?
- What do you do when your goals change or you experience setbacks?

Grades 9–12:
- How do you create meaningful and achievable goals for yourself?
- In what ways do self-assessment and peer feedback support your progress?
- How can goal setting strengthen your self-regulation and executive functioning skills?

- **Asset-Based Learning:** When we tap into students' cultural and linguistic strengths, affirm the varying ways they express their emotions, and create experiences that honor their identities, we build classrooms rich in emotional intelligence and belonging.

Grades K–2:
- What are some special ways your family or community celebrates?
- How do you feel when you share things about your culture with your classmates?
- Can you teach us a word or phrase in the language your family speaks at home?

Grades 3–5:
- How does learning about different cultures make our classroom stronger?
- What traditions or stories from your culture help you understand feelings better?
- How do you feel when your classmates show interest in your culture?

Grades 6–8:
- How does your cultural background influence how you express emotions?
- Why is it essential for us to learn about and respect diverse emotional expressions?
- How does affirming your identity and culture help your learning and relationships?

Grades 9–12:
- In what ways do cultural and linguistic assets shape your emotional intelligence?
- How can embracing diverse emotional expressions enrich our classroom community?
- What impact does identity affirmation have on your sense of belonging and well-being?

- **Classroom Inquiry:** Cooperative and collaborative learning, along with community problem-solving tasks (i.e., PBL, Service Learning), nurture collective well-being, interpersonal skills, and mutual accountability.

Grades K–2:
- How do you work with a friend to solve a problem?
- What does it mean to be helpful during group activities?
- How do you feel when your classmates listen to your ideas?

Grades 3–5:
- What role did you play in solving the group's challenge today?
- How did listening to your classmates' ideas help you think differently?
- What did you learn about working together from today's activity?

Grades 6–8:
- What strategies helped your group collaborate effectively today?
- How do you ensure everyone's voice is heard in a group task?
- Why is it important to hold yourself and your group members accountable?

Grades 9–12:
- How does collaborative inquiry strengthen your interpersonal and problem-solving skills?
- In what ways can your group approach community challenges with empathy and mutual support?
- How can accountability and shared responsibility benefit our broader community and your personal growth?

By integrating these practices, holistic learning transforms classrooms into dynamic spaces where SEL, metacognition, and executive functioning coalesce. This fosters emotionally intelligent, socially responsible learners who are ready to contribute meaningfully to their communities.

Reflect and Act

Consider this week:

How effectively does your instructional design nurture the integration of Transformational Social-Emotional Learning (tSEL), executive functioning, and metacognitive reflection?

Identify one practice to deepen emotional and cognitive synergy in your classroom:

- **Incorporate daily mindfulness practices and reflective journaling moments to enhance emotional and cognitive self-awareness.**
  - *Example (K–2):* Start each day with a short breathing exercise and ask students to draw or talk about how they feel personally and how it might help them be kind to others.

- *Example (Grades 3–12):* Begin class with a brief mindfulness activity, followed by journaling prompts like, "How do my feelings today affect me, my friends, and my classmates?"

- **Embed structured opportunities for goal setting, self-monitoring, and peer assessment to strengthen executive function and metacognitive clarity.**

  - *Example (K–2):* Students choose one simple goal each week (like helping a friend or finishing work on time), check in daily, and talk with a partner about how it went.

  - *Example (Grades 3–12):* Students set weekly personal and class goals, keep track of their progress with easy-to-use checklists, and have peer chats to share successes and challenges.

- **Design culturally responsive social-emotional practices that authentically honor and affirm diverse emotional expressions and identities.**

  - *Example (K–2):* Have students bring in or describe something special from their family or culture to share in a circle, celebrating everyone's story.

  - *Example (Grades 3–12):* Facilitate group discussions or circles in which students share stories or traditions from their cultures and discuss how understanding one another builds stronger, kinder communities.

These examples underscore the reciprocal relationship between tSEL and metacognitive awareness. Holistic approaches empower individuals to gain a deeper understanding of their thoughts, emotions, and actions, fostering compassionate decision-making and reflective engagement. Through cultivating this clarity, learners become capable of thoughtful reflection, empathetic action, and impactful contributions to their communities and beyond.

PART II:

DESIGNING FOR PRACTICE

CHAPTER 5

CLARITY OF PURPOSE

Democracy must be born anew every generation, and education is its midwife.
— **John Dewey**

Imagine standing at the edge of a bustling playground, observing two distinctly different scenes. In one corner, children diligently follow a series of prescribed tasks under the vigilant supervision of adults, each step carefully dictated but disconnected from any more profound personal significance. In another corner, students enthusiastically cluster together, engrossed in animated conversations about how best to enhance their community garden, eagerly negotiating roles and responsibilities.

1st Grade Clarity of Purpose:

In this video, first-graders at PS 9 in Staten Island, New York, practice giving peer feedback in physical education class using a clear success-criteria checklist. These students' dialogue—naming steps, offering advice, and responding with encouragement—shows how even young learners thrive when the *purpose* of the task is visible and shared. Feedback becomes more than correction; it becomes a way to clarify learning goals, strengthen relationships, and nurture agency. This is clarity of purpose in action: students know what matters, why it matters, and how to help one another grow. A casual observer might quickly label the first group as more "disciplined" or "well-behaved." However, we contend that the fundamental distinction between these two groups lies in clarity of purpose. The children, dutifully following prescribed instructions, might demonstrate compliance. Yet their actions lack a meaningful connection to their lives or a deeper personal understanding. In contrast, the second group's dynamic engagement arises directly from an authentic and shared purpose—they recognize clearly why their tasks matter and how their actions positively impact their community.

Most readers have heard (or even posed) the age-old question that surfaces in classrooms around the globe: *What relevance does this lesson have to "real life."* Metacognitive clarity flourishes when students deeply understand and connect with the purpose of their learning. When students genuinely see the relevance and value in what they are doing, they actively reflect upon, monitor, and adjust their learning processes. In classrooms rooted in democratic ideals and justice, clarity of purpose is transformative—it empowers learners to take ownership of their education, critically question existing structures, and thoughtfully engage with their world.

Yet clarity of purpose does not imply a diminished role for educators. Quite the opposite: teachers play an indispensable role by guiding students toward purposeful learning, framing meaningful questions, providing relevant examples and non-examples, and fostering reflective dialogue. This careful orchestration ensures that students develop not just compliance but also deep metacognitive clarity, rooted in purpose-driven learning experiences.

Check out the *Clarity of Purpose* section of the appendices for tools and resources, including templates, examples, and videos that will support you and your learners in this process.

High School Goal Setting Modeling:

In this video, James Milkert, world history teacher, helps students turn vague intentions into SMART goals, focusing on one clear next step at a time. By making goals specific and actionable, learners see the *purpose* of their work more clearly—why it matters and how to move forward with confidence.

Justice-Centered Learning Goals: Beyond Standards

Too often, educational goals, whether they take the form of content standards or learning intentions, become fragmented into isolated skills disconnected from real life. But genuine, justice-centered goals do something remarkable: they reintegrate learning with life, turning academic skills into powerful tools for justice, democracy, and meaningful contribution. These goals

- connect learning to real-world issues that directly impact students, families, and communities, grounding skills in democratic participation and social justice;.
- affirm and celebrate diverse identities, ensuring that every student sees their story reflected in the curriculum;
- foster critical thinking, encouraging students to question prevailing systems and imagine equitable alternatives; and
- prioritize belonging and voice, making these outcomes as essential as any academic metric.

Consider the difference between asking a student, "Can you identify the main idea?" and reframing the question as, "How can your understanding of this text amplify your voice, support your community, or spark democratic dialogue?" The shift is profound. Justice-centered clarity transforms academic standards into tools for liberation and active citizenship.

Figure 5.1: Justice-Centered Learning Goals

JUSTICE-CENTERED LEARNING GOALS

Traditional Learning Goals
- Isolated skills or standards
- Disconnected from lived experiences
- Compliance-focused
- Teacher-direted; limited agency
- Individual achievement & external rewards
- Preparation for 'real life' (abstract)

Shared Traits
- Support student growth & mastery
- Clarity about success
- Teacher guidance & feedback
- Measurable/observable outcomes
- Progress monitoring & improvement

Justice-Centered Learning Goals
- Connect skills to real-world issues
- Affirm diverse identities & voices
- Prioritize belonging & agency
- Foster criticality & questioning inequities
- Co-construction with students
- Anchor in community, contribution, criticality
- Standards as tools for justice & democracy
- Use Social Justice Standards (IDJA)

The Brain Needs Purpose

The brain is wired to care about purpose. When students take on learning that feels meaningful, especially work connected to justice or their own lives, the brain lights up in powerful ways. Reward centers like the ventral striatum and orbitofrontal cortex kick into gear, boosting motivation and sharpening focus (Diamond, 2013; Immordino-Yang & Damasio, 2007).

Interestingly, offering external rewards, like money, grades, or praise, can actually backfire. When students focus on the reward instead of the reason, their intrinsic drive fades. But when learning feels like it is theirs—self-directed, purposeful, and real—the brain's internal reward system steps in, sustaining curiosity from the inside out (Murayama et al., 2010).

Justice-Centered Learning Goals Across Content Areas

These goals ensure learning is authentically connected to life, promoting academic excellence through the lens of justice, belonging, and democratic participation.

English Language Arts: Theme Analysis

- **Traditional Goal:** Can you determine the theme of a story?
- **Justice-Centered Goal:**
  - How can analyzing themes in literature deepen your understanding of social justice, amplify marginalized voices, or inspire actions that strengthen your community?
  - How can identifying themes in literature help you better understand the strengths, histories, and challenges within our school community, and empower you to actively contribute to making our school a more inclusive, supportive, and equitable environment?

Mathematics: Data Representation

- **Traditional Goal:** Can you create and interpret graphs?
- **Justice-Centered Goals:**
  - How can visually representing and interpreting data empower you to identify inequities in our school, advocate for fairness among classmates, and amplify the perspectives of students whose voices need to be heard?
  - How can representing and interpreting data visually empower you to expose injustice, advocate for fairness, or amplify voices in your community that need to be heard?

Social Studies: Historical Analysis

- **Traditional Goal:** Can you analyze the causes and effects of historical events?
- **Justice-Centered Goals:**
  - How can critically analyzing historical events help you recognize patterns of inequity within our school community, advocate for peers whose voices might be overlooked, and actively participate in making our school a more inclusive and just environment?
  - How can critically analyzing historical events equip you to recognize patterns of inequity, advocate for marginalized communities, and actively contribute to a more just society?

Science: Environmental Responsibility

- **Traditional Goal:** Can you describe human impacts on ecosystems?
- **Justice-Centered Goals:**

- How does understanding human impacts on ecosystems enable you to take informed actions toward environmental justice within our school community and advocate for sustainable practices that promote a healthier campus environment?
- How does understanding human impacts on ecosystems enable you to take informed action toward environmental justice and advocate for sustainable practices in your community?

Visual Arts: Artistic Expression

- **Traditional Goal:** Can you create art using various techniques?
- **Justice-Centered Goals:**

  - How can your artistic creations celebrate the diverse identities within our school community, challenge stereotypes or unfair narratives, and inspire meaningful conversations about inclusion, social change, and justice among your peers and teachers?
  - How can your artistic creations celebrate diverse identities, challenge oppressive narratives, and provoke dialogue about social change and justice?

Music: Cultural Appreciation

- **Traditional Goal:** Can you recognize and perform musical styles from various cultures?
- **Justice-Centered Goals:**

  - How can engaging with diverse musical traditions within our school community build empathy among students and staff, break down cultural biases, and elevate voices that have been historically silenced or marginalized in our school and in the wider world?
  - How can engaging with diverse musical traditions impact your understanding and appreciation of cultures that are different from your own?

Physical Education: Teamwork and Collaboration

- **Traditional Goal:** Can you demonstrate effective teamwork in physical activities?
- **Justice-Centered Goal:**

  - How can practicing teamwork and collaboration build inclusive relationships, value diverse perspectives, and promote equity both inside and outside of your school community?

World Languages: Cultural Communication

- **Traditional Goal:** Can you effectively communicate basic information in another language?
- **Justice-Centered Goals:**

- How does communicating across languages and cultures enhance your ability to advocate for inclusion, challenge stereotypes, and create spaces of belonging?
- How does communicating across languages and cultures within your friend group enhance your ability to promote inclusion, challenge stereotypes, and foster a sense of belonging among your friends?

Health: Personal Wellness

- **Traditional Goal:** Can you identify strategies for personal health?
- **Justice-Centered Goals**:
    - How can understanding wellness and practicing self-care empower you to make informed decisions about your own health, develop resilience, and strengthen your overall well-being?
    - How can understanding wellness and self-care equip you to advocate for equitable access to health resources, address systemic disparities, and strengthen your community's collective well-being?

Deepening Goals Through Social Justice Standards

To effectively ground justice-centered goals in both academic rigor and democratic values, educators can leverage the Social Justice Standards, a comprehensive anti-bias framework emphasizing identity, diversity, justice, and action (IDJA). These standards explicitly support students in developing positive social identities, cultivating respect for diversity, critically analyzing injustice, and taking informed collective action. Incorporating these standards strengthens educational practices by ensuring that goals are part of a coherent vision for building inclusive, reflective, and equitable learning communities. The standards, which can be applied to all grade levels and content areas, provide practical pathways and age-appropriate outcomes, guiding students to connect their academic learning with real-world democratic participation and social transformation (Learning for Justice, 2016).

Refer to *Integrating Academic Standards With Social Justice Standards* and *From Standards to Justice: Using AI to Center Equity in Learning Goals* for a straightforward process and detailed examples illustrating the integration of these standards. Both tools are found in the Learning Tools for Clarity of Purpose appendices under the heading *Identity, Justice, and Belonging as Foundations*.

Co-Constructing Learning Pathways With Students

As we've emphasized previously, the heart of democracy in education is student agency. In democratic classrooms, students not only know their goals but play an active role in defining or "co-constructing" them. Imagine a classroom in which learners negotiate the criteria for success, linking their goals to their identities, passions, and dreams. Co-construction is a dynamic dance between students and teachers, with each bringing their strengths and perspectives to the process.

In this co-construction process, teachers play a pivotal role when they

- engage students in open discussions about why learning matters and connecting it to their lives,
- provide high-quality examples and non-examples to guide students in identifying essential success criteria,
- utilize strategic questioning to help students uncover and articulate the success criteria embedded within provided examples, and
- offer key criteria that students may overlook, ensuring clarity and rigor in the learning goals.

Students contribute actively when they

- explore and articulate how learning goals resonate with their personal experiences and aspirations;
- collaboratively analyze provided examples and nonexamples to define clear and meaningful success criteria;
- make informed choices about topics, projects, and methods that align with their interests and maintain rigorous standards;
- define excellence through their unique perspectives, thereby taking ownership of their learning outcomes; and
- regularly revisit and refine goals through collaborative reflection, ensuring education remains dynamic and responsive.

When students engage in co-construction, they experience a sense of genuine ownership, deep engagement, and a vibrant, responsive learning environment.

Educators who provide opportunities for student voice and choice nurture student agency and the capacity to co-construct learning pathways. For example, imagine an English class in which students choose novels reflective of their lived experiences, and choose between various modalities to demonstrate their learning, including written essays, podcasts, or visual presentations. Or a science class, where students create experiments addressing local environmental concerns like water quality, and jointly set criteria for successful inquiry. In mathematics, learners might also tackle community-specific problems—for example, making recommendations to the city council on the numbers of affordable housing units to build over the next five years. In the process, they work together to collaboratively define "rigor" and "precision." Even physical education students can co-design fitness goals to meet real community needs—perhaps establishing a walking club for local seniors. When students help design their pathways, the message is clear: your voice matters, your ideas shape your learning, and your education equips you to change your world.

Anchoring Learning in Community, Contribution, and Criticality

True educational purpose transcends individual achievement. It becomes transformative when anchored in community well-being, meaningful contribution, and critical thinking (see Figure 5.2). These pillars encourage students to perceive their learning not just as personal advancement but as a collective responsibility.

Figure 5.2: Anchoring Learning

Community

Essential anchoring question:

How does this learning strengthen our connections and shared humanity?

Contribution

Essential anchoring question:

How can this knowledge empower me to positively impact my family, school, and broader community?

Criticality

Essential anchoring question:

Which assumptions, inequities, or structures of power must I challenge with what I'm learning?

These questions find powerful expression across disciplines:

- In **ELA,** students explore how literature reflects social justice issues, advocate for solutions, and critically analyze biases.
- **Science** learners investigate environmental injustices, design sustainable community solutions, and challenge inequitable systems.
- **Social studies** students engage in critical discussions of whether the rights granted to Americans in the U.S. Constitution hold true today.
- **Mathematics** classes use data analysis to identify and address disparities, challenging systemic inequities through quantitative reasoning.
- **Physical education** explores community access disparities, empowering students to advocate for equitable health resources.
- **Art students** confront societal injustices through creative expression, actively using art to challenge norms and champion equity.

Education, anchored in these values, becomes less about individual rewards and more about collective flourishing, equipping learners to become thoughtful stewards of a democratic society.

Resources like the *Community Impact Project Planner* and the *Interactive Community Impact Bulletin Board* make the connection to purpose crystal clear for students and the community. These and more are housed in the Learing Tools for Clarity of Purpose under the heading *Purpose-Driven Reflection and Action*.

Clarity as a Democratic Act

We won't achieve clarity of purpose, rooted deeply in justice and democracy, by simply reiterating or paraphrasing content standards. Our students deserve nothing less than a leap of faith in which we commit to student agency, voice, and liberation. In doing so, we genuinely trust our students to make meaning and enact change; we humanize our learning communities.

In these vibrant, democratic spaces, education is no mere rehearsal for life but rather it is life itself, rich with purpose, connectedness, and an unwavering pursuit of justice.

Reflect and Act

This week, reflect: How explicitly do your learning goals connect academic skills to real-world justice, community engagement, and meaningful contribution?

Choose one deliberate action to bring clarity of purpose to life:

- Co-construct success criteria with students and use them for peer feedback (like the PS 09 first graders).
- Reframe a traditional goal into a justice-centered one that matters to students' lives.
- Anchor a current unit in community, contribution, or criticality to make purpose visible.

Clarity of purpose flourishes when students see *why their learning matters*—to themselves, their peers, and the world.

CHAPTER 6

CLARITY OF PROCESS: ILLUMINATING THE INVISIBLE PATH

We do not learn from experience . . . we learn from reflecting on experience.
— **John Dewey**

Long before the invention of GPS, sailors on open seas relied on stars and constellations to guide their voyages. Clarity of process is like these constellations, but rather than points of light (many of which were transmitted millions of years ago), think of the stars as navigational steps toward meaningful learning. If clarity of purpose is our North Star, anchoring learning in justice and democracy, clarity of process is the network of constellations we chart together.

Check out the *Learning Tools for Clarity of Process* section of the appendices for tools and resources, including templates, examples, and videos that will support you and your learners in this process.

The Art of Explicitly Teaching Learning-to-Learn

In classrooms designed to cultivate lifelong learners, it's not sufficient to simply tell students what to learn. True mastery emerges when students are explicitly taught *how* to learn—transforming learning itself into a deliberate and strategic pursuit.

Metacognitive strategies provide a framework for thinking about one's own thinking. They encompass the metacognitive cycle (see Figure 6.1):

- **Plan:** Decide how to approach a learning task
- **Monitor:** Track comprehension and evaluate progress during tasks
- **Evaluate:** Reflect afterward to gauge effectiveness and identify areas for improvement

Figure 6.1: The Metacognitive Cycle

METACOGNITIVE CYCLE

PLAN
- Set a clear goal
- Analyze a model
- Co-construct success criteria
- Choose strategies and tools
- Schedule checkpoints

MONITOR
- Check against success criteria
- Collect quick evidence
- Use self-talk or partner feedback
- Adjust strategies, time, or supports

EVALUATE
- Compare final work to success criteria/model
- Name what strategies/conditions worked & why
- Identify growth and needs
- Set next steps: revise, practice, or extend

Within this broader metacognitive framework, learning-to-learn strategies specifically target a student's ability to manage their own learning processes effectively. These strategies include

- setting meaningful goals and reflecting on progress;
- strategic planning for learning tasks;
- ongoing self-monitoring and self-assessment;

- peer assessment and collaborative feedback;
- revision and refinement based on feedback;
- note-taking, summarizing, and synthesizing information; and
- effective time management and organizational skills.

MLL SELF & PEER ASSESSMENT:

In this video, multilingual learner (MLL) students at PS 16 in Staten Island use a color-coded continuum to self- and peer-assess their writing. By making proficiency levels visible, the continuum transforms assessment into process clarity: students see where they are, where they're headed, and what steps to take next. This concrete tool makes learning-to-learn strategies, self-monitoring, peer feedback, and revision tangible and empowering, especially for multilingual learners.

Keep in mind that not all metacognitive strategies exclusively target learning itself; some extend into broader cognitive processes like problem-solving, decision-making, or critical thinking (Hattie & Donoghue, 2016). Specifically, learning-to-learn strategies equip students to regulate, optimize, and enhance their own learning processes. Think of these strategies as essential gear for a learner's journey, providing tools for reflective inquiry, meaningful self-assessment, and critical reflection. They make learning visible and accessible by positioning students as active agents in their educational journeys.

Goal Setting: Goals that connect personal mastery to communal justice sharpen students' purpose.
- **ELA:** A student intentionally seeks diverse perspectives for their research paper, amplifying voices that often go unheard.
- **Social Studies:** Students commit to interviewing varied community members, ensuring inclusive narratives in local histories.

Strategic Planning: Breaking complexity down into clarity, ensuring no learner feels lost.
- **Science:** Students carefully map each stage of an environmental experiment, transforming overwhelming tasks into manageable actions.
- **Art:** When creating a mural, students outline clear timelines and responsibilities, embodying democratic collaboration.

Ongoing Self-Monitoring: Self-questioning turns every learner into their own reflective coach.
- **Math:** Mid-problem check-ins help students recalibrate their strategies, refining their reasoning continuously.
- **ELA:** Students use monitoring bookmarks to pause, reflect, and adapt their understanding of challenging texts.

Reflective Evaluation: Reflection that isn't just an endpoint but a launchpad for deeper insights (Flavell, 1976).

- **Science:** Students revisit their hypotheses post-investigation, tracing how their thinking evolved through evidence.
- **Physical Education:** Students regularly assess their fitness journeys, identifying adjustments needed for sustained success.

Like most cognitively demanding tasks, learning to learn takes time and persistence. Educators can guide students beyond a surface-level knowledge of learning to learn strategies through deliberate practice across various contexts. This comprehensive approach ensures students internalize these tools, fostering deeper engagement, heightened self-awareness, and an enduring capacity to adapt and thrive both within and beyond the classroom.

Check out our *Learning-to-Learn Strategy Guide* under the heading *Navigating the Metacognitive Cycle in the Learning Tools* for Clarify of Purpose for additional explicit strategies for helping students become more aware of their thinking and learning processes.

Weaving Metacognition Into Every Moment

Great teachers know that clarity of process can't simply be tacked onto lessons; it must be seamlessly integrated. The metacognitive cycle is most powerful when it's an organic, ongoing part of the learning experience.

Start With Planning Prompts (Before the Task)

Planning prompts guide students before beginning tasks, helping them select effective strategies, anticipate obstacles, and set clear goals for their learning.

Selecting Strategies:

- What strategies have worked well for you before in similar tasks?
- Which strategies do you think will best support your understanding today?
- Why are you choosing this approach, and how will it help you accomplish your goal?
- How might you approach this differently than in the past?

Anticipating Obstacles:

- What challenges or roadblocks might you encounter?
- What resources or supports can you identify ahead of time to help you overcome these challenges?

- If your initial approach doesn't work, what alternative strategy might you try?
- What specific questions could you ask if you get stuck?

Setting Goals:

- What exactly do you hope to achieve or learn today?
- How will you know if you're successful during the task?
- What might success feel like or look like at different points during this activity?
- How can this learning contribute to your overall growth or community impact?

Check out *Student Planning Prompt Cards* as well as a set for *Monitoring* and *Evaluating* for reproducible prompts and examples to support learners in the planning phase. Both are housed in the Learning Tools for Clarity of Purpose under the heading *Prompting Metacognitive Thinking*.

Midway Monitoring Check-Ins (During the Task)

Midway monitoring check-ins prompt students to pause during tasks, reflect on their progress, evaluate strategy effectiveness, and adjust their approach as needed to achieve their learning goals.

Strategy Effectiveness Checks:

- How well is your chosen strategy working right now?
- What evidence do you have that you're progressing toward your goal?
- Are there any adjustments or shifts in your approach needed at this point?
- Is there another strategy that might work better given your current understanding?

Emotional and Motivational Checks:

- How are you feeling about your progress? Why?
- What's working well, and what feels difficult right now?
- Are you experiencing any confusion or frustration? How can we address that together?
- What small step can you take next to maintain or boost your motivation?

Collaboration and Support Checks:

- Have you connected with peers or used available resources effectively?
- Is there anyone whose perspective or input might enhance your understanding at this point?
- How has collaboration helped or hindered your learning so far?

Reflection Builds Neural Flexibility

When students pause to evaluate their progress and adjust strategies mid-task, they strengthen the brain's prefrontal cortex. This helps them become more flexible, persistent learners who can revise their approach when things get challenging (Zelazo & Lyons, 2012).

Post-Task Evaluations (After the Task)

Conclude activities with reflective dialogue, reinforcing growth and guiding future strategy use.

Reflective Dialogue and Learning:

- Which strategies were most effective, and why do you think they worked?
- What strategies did you try today that you might use again in the future?
- If you could repeat this task, what would you do differently and why?
- How did your initial predictions about challenges align with your actual experience?

Growth and Progress Reinforcement:

- What new insights about your learning style or process did you gain today?
- How does today's learning connect to broader personal, academic, or community goals?
- Can you identify a strength you demonstrated during this activity? How might you build on this strength moving forward?

Forward-Thinking and Application:

- How can what you learned today help you tackle future tasks or challenges?
- What new strategies or skills do you want to further develop or explore?
- What remaining questions do you have, and how can we explore them together?

Student Self-Reflection:

In this video, students at PS 65 in Staten Island demonstrate how structured reflection builds both academic clarity and social-emotional awareness. By naming their learning strategies and emotions aloud, they connect self-monitoring to personal growth and community contribution—making the invisible process of learning visible and empowering.

Post-task reflection is a skill that extends far beyond classrooms and schools. We live in an era in which misinformation spreads faster than truth. When students pause to ask, *"Did this information come from a trustworthy source?"* or *"Was I emotionally swayed, or did I analyze critically?"* they aren't just evaluating their work. They are, more importantly, developing the discernment necessary for responsible citizenship. Teaching learners to reflect on source reliability, emotional influence, and logical coherence deepens their metacognitive toolkit and fortifies them against manipulation in a post-truth world. Refer to more prompts for detecting misinformation in the next section.

Reflection Builds a Flexible Brain

Thinking isn't just about getting answers—it's about staying adaptable. When students reflect on how they're learning, not just what they're learning, they strengthen the part of the brain responsible for flexible thinking and problem-solving. These check-ins—"What worked?" and "What will I do differently next time?"—light up the prefrontal cortex, building the mental muscle needed to shift gears and try new strategies (Diamond, 2013; Zelazo & Lyons, 2012).

Additional Prompts for Deepening Metacognitive Clarity

Additional prompts for deepening metacognitive clarity encourage students to explicitly articulate their thought processes, critically analyze their approaches, and connect their learning to civics, equity, identity, and community engagement.

Prompts for Detecting Misinformation:

- What makes this source trustworthy—or not?
  - *Who created it? Are they an expert, biased, or trying to persuade me?*
- How is this information making me feel—and why?
  - *Am I reacting with anger, fear, or outrage? Could that be intentional?*
- What evidence is this claim based on?
  - *Does it include facts, data, or sources I can verify—or just opinions and emotion?*
- What perspectives are missing from this story or post?
  - *Whose voices are left out? How might that shape what I'm being told?*
- Have I cross-checked this information with another reliable source?
  - *What do other credible outlets or experts say about this topic?*

Prompts for Articulating Thinking:
- Can you describe step-by-step how you arrived at your answer or solution?
- What mental images or metaphors helped you understand this topic?
- How clearly can you explain your thinking process to someone else?

Prompts for Critical and Analytical Thinking:
- Which parts of the task required deeper thinking or analysis? Why?
- How did questioning your assumptions or rethinking your approach help your learning today?
- Were there points where challenging your own thinking led to new insights?

Prompts for Equity, Belonging, and Justice:
- How did your learning today affirm or connect to your personal identity or experiences?
- In what ways can the skills you learned today help you advocate for yourself or others?
- How can you apply today's learning to engage more meaningfully in your community or the world around you?

Prompts for Civic Reflection and Democratic Engagement:
- How does this learning help me better understand my role in a community or democracy?
- What issue or injustice would I like to change—and what knowledge or skills might help me do that?
- Whose voices or experiences do I need to understand better to make fair decisions or take informed action?
- How can I use what I've learned to collaborate with others and create positive change?
- What does responsible participation (in school, online, or in my community) look like for me today?

Across Disciplines to Strengthen Metacognitive Clarity

Prompts across disciplines to strengthen metacognitive clarity involve consistently embedding reflective practices within all subject areas to help students become more self-aware, strategic learners.

- **ELA:** Students pause during essay drafts to assess the alignment of their evidence and claims.
- **Science:** Hypothesis adjustments are explicitly documented, revealing the dynamic nature of scientific inquiry.
- **Social Studies:** Learners reflect on their shifting views after examining primary historical documents.
- **Math:** Problem-solving errors are leveraged as opportunities to explore multiple approaches.

- **World Languages:** Students regularly reflect on language strategies that aid their comprehension and fluency, adjusting techniques based on conversational success.
- **Visual and Performing Arts:** Learners evaluate their artistic choices mid-project, articulating how adjustments to their technique or expression influence the quality of their work.
- **Physical Education:** Students monitor their performance during activities, assessing the effectiveness of strategies for teamwork, skills improvement, and overall physical goals.
- **Career and Technical Education (CTE):** Students analyze decision-making processes during hands-on projects, refining skills and techniques based on real-time feedback and outcomes.
- **Health Education:** Students pause during activities to reflect on personal wellness strategies, examining their effectiveness in managing stress or promoting healthy habits.
- **Advisory:** Students regularly journal or dialogue about how their personal goals align with their academic strategies, monitoring growth in self-awareness and decision-making.

Navigate to the heading *Content-Specific Tools for Metacognitive Practice* within the Learning Tools for Clarity of Processs to download *Discipline-Specific Metacognitive Tools* and *Metacognitive Clarity in the Subject Areas*. Both resources expand on these ideas and offer examples and explanations to support your work in the classroom.

Making the Invisible Visible

Clarity of process can also be described as making our thinking visible—a learned skill that requires disciplined practice. Teachers can support this learning by applying any of the following strategies.

1. **Thinking Routines:**
   - **See-Think-Wonder:** Encourages students to observe carefully (See), interpret thoughtfully (Think), and explore questions that spark curiosity (Wonder), fostering deeper critical inquiry.
   - **Claim-Support-Question:** Promotes structured thinking by having students state ideas (Claim), provide evidence or reasons (Support), and identify areas needing further exploration (Question), enhancing evidence-based reasoning.
   - **Connect-Extend-Challenge:** Helps learners link new ideas to existing knowledge (Connect), expand their understanding through fresh insights (Extend), and actively question or problematize concepts (Challenge), thus continually advancing their intellectual growth.
2. **Student-Generated Success Criteria:** Students collaborate to create rubrics that clearly define what high-quality work looks like, integrating rigorous academic standards with

democratic principles such as student voice, teamwork, and real-world significance. For example, a class might design a rubric for a persuasive essay that includes criteria like clarity of argument, incorporation of peer feedback, and relevance to community issues.

3. **Learning Journals:** Students maintain ongoing journals that document their thinking, strategies, reflections, and moments of insight throughout their learning journey. For instance, after solving math problems, students might reflect on strategies they used, challenges they encountered, questions that arose, and how their thinking evolved—making their metacognitive processes transparent and accessible.

4. **Dialogue Protocols:** Protocols such as Socratic Seminars or Collaborative Reasoning Circles guide structured conversations that encourage students to articulate and examine their reasoning openly. For example, in a Socratic Seminar about a historical event, students actively question and respond to each other's interpretations, creating a shared understanding while valuing multiple, diverse viewpoints.

5. **Discipline-Specific Strategies:** Each discipline employs specialized techniques to reveal and enhance student thinking. For example, in ELA, comprehension-monitoring strategies encourage students to verbalize their interpretive processes, making their reading comprehension visible. In Science, hypothesis maps visually capture students' evolving theories, highlighting the dynamic and iterative nature of scientific inquiry. Within Social Studies, evidence webs explicitly link claims to multiple and diverse sources, promoting rigorous historical reasoning. In Math, open-ended problem-solving tasks invite students to share multiple solution pathways, showcasing varied mathematical approaches and deepening collective understanding.

When educators intentionally embed these strategies, classrooms become vibrant, transparent communities of learning where each student's intellectual process is celebrated and leveraged to enrich collective understanding. This commitment to visibility not only democratizes the learning experience but also cultivates deeper engagement, sustained curiosity, and lasting critical thinking skills.

High School Feedback on Feedback:

In this video, American Studies students at Lyons Township High School engage in peer assessment of literary analysis while their teacher, Virginia Condon, listens in and offers "feedback on feedback." By modeling and refining the process in real time, she ensures that peer assessment is both reliable and meaningful. This is clarity of process in action—making the steps of giving and receiving feedback visible so students learn *how* to learn together with quality and precision.

Honoring the Journey

Clarity of process is foundational to fostering genuine learning-to-learn capabilities. It ensures students explicitly understand, practice, and reflect upon their cognitive strategies.

This chapter emphasizes that when students gain clarity in goal setting, strategic planning, self-monitoring, and reflective evaluation, they are empowered to take deliberate ownership of their learning journeys. Such clarity transforms classrooms into democratic spaces where each learner's unique thinking processes are acknowledged, honored, and developed. Ultimately, clarity of process nurtures lifelong learners who possess the confidence, self-awareness, and adaptability to navigate diverse challenges, extending their transformative influence far beyond school walls. Clarity of process is justice in action.

Progressions of Metacognitive Clarity

The *Metacognitive Clarity Progressions Metacognitive Clarity Progressions with Evidence Menu Connections* maps how learners demonstrate planning, monitoring, and evaluating as they move from surface to deep to transfer levels. Table 6.1 highlights the K–2 progression, showing how our youngest learners take greater ownership of strategies, feedback, and goal setting. (See the full K–12 Progression in the Learning Tools for Clarity of Process online appendices under the heading *Navigating the Metacognitive Cycle*.)

Table 6.1: K–2 Metacognitive Clarity Progression with Evidence Menu Connections

Level of Clarity	Phase of Cycle	Look-Fors (What Learners Do)	Listen-Fors (What Learners Say)	Evidence Menu Connections (Observable Indicators)
Surface	Plan	Point to visuals or models when describing thinking. Sort work into "done" versus "not yet." Use sentence frames to share strategy choice.	*I tried it this way . . . I used counting on. I need help with . . .*	Percentage of students naming at least one strategy. Students use teacher-provided rubric language in conferences. Evidence of reflection sentence frames in journals.
Deep	Monitor	Compare strategies with peers. Explain why a strategy worked or didn't. Begin self-assessment with the criteria.	*I used this because . . . Her way worked better because . . . I met this goal, but still need to . . .*	Quality of "because" reasoning in peer talk. Students identify success criteria without prompting. Percentage of learners revising work after feedback.
Transfer	Evaluate	Apply strategies to new tasks. Choose goals beyond teacher direction. Use peer/teacher feedback to plan next steps.	*I can use this for my story too. Next time I'll . . . I set a goal to . . .*	Students generate their own goals during reflection. Unprompted use of rubric language. Evidence of transfer in student-led conferences.

Reflect and Act

Reflect: How intentionally do you embed clarity of process, goal setting, strategic planning, self-monitoring, and reflective evaluation into daily learning? The Metacognitive Clarity Progressions show what these processes look and sound like as learners grow from surface to deep to transfer levels. In this chapter, we've highlighted the Grades 6–8 progression to illustrate how students begin to take greater ownership of their strategies, feedback, and goal setting. The full K–12 progression is available in the Online Appendices for your use as a reference tool.

Act: Identify one practice in your classroom where making the invisible processes of thinking visible could strengthen student agency and democratic participation, and commit to one deliberate action:

- Explicitly teach and regularly integrate learning-to-learn strategies into classroom routines.
- Systematically embed planning, monitoring, and evaluating prompts into instruction, encouraging students to openly share their thought processes.
- Use the progressions to notice, name, and celebrate students' growth in metacognitive clarity over time.

Cultivating clarity of process as a democratic practice empowers students to become strategic, reflective learners, capable of shaping their educational journeys and contributing meaningfully to their communities.

CHAPTER 7

CLARITY OF OWNERSHIP

The most effective learning communities are those where learners are genuinely at the helm, shaping their own educational journeys.
— The Authors

Think about the following question: Who "owns" your learning?

In the context of education, ownership reflects something that resonates at the core of democratic values: voice, agency, and collective responsibility. Clarity of ownership calls for a bold reshaping of traditional, teacher-centered models of teaching and learning in which our students are akin to baby birds, just waiting to be fed regurgitated knowledge. Rather than quiet spaces where compliant students passively receive information, imagine classrooms that are vibrant forums where students actively shape their learning paths through dialogue, reflection, and shared decision-making. The classroom, in this sense, becomes a microcosm of democracy itself.

But let's be clear: democratic ownership doesn't happen by accident. It emerges from intentional, structured practices designed to give students genuine control—student-led reflection, collaborative assessment, and student-driven goal setting. These practices turn learners into active participants, cultivating the mindset and skills essential not just for academic success but also for engaged citizenship.

Check out the *Learning Tools for Clarity of Ownership* online appendices starting for tools and resources, including templates, examples, and videos that will support you and your learners in this process.

Student-Led Reflection, Co-Assessment, and Goal Setting

When students take the lead in reflection, assessment, and goal setting, education becomes a vibrant dialogue rather than a passive exchange. Imagine a classroom where learners actively question, critique, and reconstruct their understanding, transforming every experience into a catalyst for deeper learning. In such spaces, students don't merely consume spoon-fed knowledge but interact dynamically with it, building self-awareness and fostering a profound sense of agency.

Together, student-led reflection, co-assessment, and goal setting are part of the formative assessment process that makes learning visible and actionable, illustrated in Figure 7.1. Rather than isolated strategies, these practices operate as a continuous cycle in which learners clarify goals and success criteria, engage in self and peer assessment, reflect on evidence of learning, and set ambitious next steps. Questioning, discussion, and feedback fuel the process, enabling students to monitor progress, adjust strategies, and take increasing ownership of their learning over time.

Figure 7.1: The Formative Assessment Process

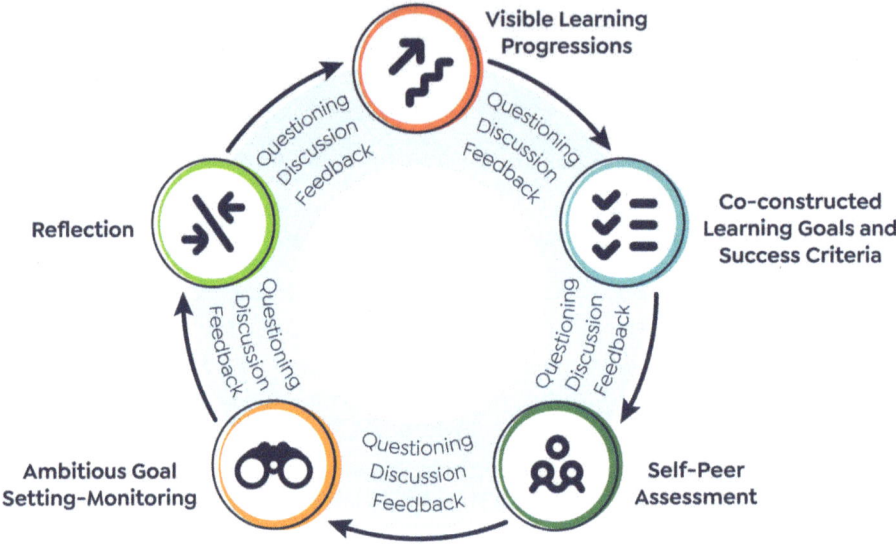

Reflection

Reflection is an ongoing conversation students have with themselves, not just a final thought. Reflective learners don't just absorb; they engage, dissect, and reconstruct knowledge.

7th Grade Math Reflection:

See It in Action: Listen in as these seventh-grade math students reflect on their work and thinking. The Core Collaborative YouTube page has many more videos of learners reflecting.

Examples:

- **Language Arts:** Reflective journals document not just what students learned but how their approach to learning evolved.
- **Mathematics:** Exit tickets capture daily reflections, prompting students to question their methods.
- **Science:** Peer-led discussions after experiments drive deeper inquiry and collective improvements.

Co-Assessment

Co-assessment amplifies reflection by shifting power from teachers alone to a shared dialogue among students. Research, primarily in higher education, demonstrates that peer assessment promotes metacognitive growth, increases engagement and motivation, strengthens communication and social skills, and fosters openness to diverse perspectives (Falchikov, 2005; Topping, 1998). Through collaborative assessment, learners develop collective accountability, deepen their understanding of success, and participate more actively in democratic learning communities (Bloomberg & Pitchford, 2023).

5th Grade Peer Assessment:

See It in Action: Begin your journey with these fifth-grade students engaged in peer assessment of their summary writing. The Core Collaborative YouTube page has dozens more related videos.

Examples:

- **Social Studies:** Peer-assessing group presentations using rubrics they helped design by analyzing and discussing quality presentations.
- **Visual Arts:** Gallery walks guided by success criteria students created together with their teacher, anchored in the larger goals of the unit.
- **Physical Education:** Students use self-developed checklists to assess teamwork in group sports.

Goal Setting

Student-driven goal setting shifts the educational compass from external demands to personal aspirations. Goals students set for themselves are inherently meaningful, personal, and compelling.

Examples:

- **World Languages:** Personalized goals tracked via language portfolios.
- **Music Education:** Performance targets monitored through recordings and reflective journals.
- **Technology:** Project-specific coding or digital design goals are revisited regularly through reflective dialogue.

By placing students at the heart of reflection, assessment, and goal setting, educators create empowered learners who actively shape their educational journeys. These practices not only deepen academic understanding but also cultivate essential democratic skills, preparing students to navigate complex challenges with confidence and purpose.

See It in Action - HS Riskometer:

In this video, teachers Kim Molloy and Samantha Sahota from Naples Street Elementary (PS 9, District 31 in Staten Island, New York) share how they have adapted Guy Claxton's Riskometer to help students reflect on their confidence and readiness to take risks. By naming how they feel, students practice the metacognitive moves of monitoring and adjusting, while also strengthening trust with peers and teachers. This empathetic approach has opened opportunities for choice, supported achievement, and built confidence, showing how reflection tools can deepen ownership of learning.

Elevating Learner Voice in Shaping Success Criteria

Imagine a scenario where success criteria aren't simply delivered, they're debated, redefined, and personally meaningful because students had a hand in crafting them. Authentic student involvement isn't optional; it's essential.

To effectively elevate learner voice, educators should:

- Introduce real-world, high-quality examples and model critical thinking aloud.
- Offer both traditional and unconventional examples to expand perceptions of success.
- Ensure success criteria remain fluid and adaptable, inviting continual student input.

Teacher prompts:

- "What stands out as effective about these examples?"
- "How do we avoid common pitfalls shown in these non-examples?"
- "How can our criteria celebrate both traditional and innovative paths?"

Student reflections:

- "What specifically makes this example resonate with me?"
- "How does my identity influence my view of successful work?"»
- "What unique strength or innovation can I add?"

When learners see their voices genuinely shaping what success looks like, ownership moves beyond theory, and it becomes tangible, vibrant, and personal.

Moving to co-construction and the ongoing revision of success criteria can feel like a significant shift. Check out the *Success Criteria Co-Creation Protocol* and *Success Criteria Refinement Template* in the Learning Tools for Clarity of Ownership appendices under the heading *Co-Construction of Success Criteria and Assessment* to smooth the transition or for new ideas if you're already engaging in co-construction.

Elementatry Reflection on Success Criteria:

In this video, an elementary student from PS 48 in Staten Island, New York, explains how a color-coded continuum with success criteria helps her self-monitor and reflect on her growth over the school year. By making expectations visible, the continuum turns assessment into a clear process: students see where they are, where they're going, and how to chart their next steps with purpose.

Continuous Refinement and Innovation in Success Criteria

Static success criteria limit potential. Real-world success is dynamic, fluid, and adaptive. Educators must embrace continuous refinement driven by ongoing student reflection and feedback. This iterative process ensures criteria remain meaningful, relevant, and inclusive of diverse perspectives. As Gottlieb (2016) emphasizes, assessment criteria should be negotiated with learners, especially multilingual students, taking into account both language and modality. Depending on the learning intention, translanguaging or the use of home languages may be entirely appropriate, and alternative modes such as drawings, oral explanations, or video clips can be just as valid as written text in demonstrating mastery.

Examples:

- **English Literature:** Students regularly revisit essay rubrics, incorporating peer insights and reflections to better align with evolving writing skills and styles.
- **Science Projects:** Success criteria for experiments are continuously refined based on student feedback after each lab, adapting to new discoveries and innovative approaches.
- **History Debates:** Debate evaluation criteria are adjusted in response to student suggestions, ensuring they remain relevant and inclusive of diverse argumentation styles.
- **Mathematics Problem-Solving:**
  Students collaboratively refine success criteria for complex math problems by reflecting on the clarity of explanations and diversity of problem-solving methods shared in class, continuously improving how mathematical reasoning is assessed.
- **Visual Arts Portfolios:**
  Criteria for evaluating portfolios evolve as students provide feedback on creativity, cultural representation, and personal expression, ensuring the criteria authentically capture diverse artistic visions.
- **Physical Education Goals:**
  Fitness and skill benchmarks are revisited frequently, allowing students to integrate personal health reflections, evolving fitness priorities, and inclusive approaches that consider varied abilities and goals.
- **World Language Presentations:**
  Criteria for oral presentations in a new language adapt continually based on student reflections about effective communication strategies, cultural responsiveness, and evolving fluency levels, ensuring criteria remain authentic and meaningful.

The Power of Success Criteria:

In this video, a student shares how success criteria became a part of his learning journey. By naming their value in his own words, he illustrates how ownership of success criteria is not abstract—it shapes daily choices, strengthens reflection, and makes learning goals visible and attainable.

Cultivating Habits of Mind for Deeper Ownership

Habits of Mind are foundational dispositions students rely upon to genuinely take ownership of their learning journeys. Developed by Costa and Kallick (2008), these 16 habits equip learners with essential cognitive, emotional, and social competencies critical for sustained academic success and lifelong learning. These habits nurture resilience, critical reflection, and adaptability, providing learners with powerful tools to confidently navigate academic and real-world challenges.

Explicitly cultivating Habits of Mind in classrooms amplifies student-led reflection, co-assessment, and goal setting. They reinforce democratic educational structures by fostering deeper cognitive engagement, enhancing emotional regulation, and nurturing meaningful collaboration (Bloomberg & Pitchford, 2023; Hammond, 2015). Each habit empowers students to intentionally and thoughtfully control their educational experiences.

Purpose Strengthens Self-Regulation

When students set meaningful, self-driven goals, they activate neural systems that help them stay motivated and manage their learning. These brain pathways also support persistence and flexible problem-solving (Zelazo & Lyons, 2012).Integrating Habits of Mind Into Democratic Ownership

The 16 Habits of Mind identified by Art Costa and Bena Kallick (2008) each uniquely strengthen student ownership by providing practical pathways for intentional, reflective action:

1. **Persisting:** Sustained effort in pursuing challenging goals.
2. **Managing Impulsivity:** Thoughtful responses rather than reactive behaviors.
3. **Listening With Understanding and Empathy:** Active listening to deeply understand others' perspectives.
4. **Thinking Flexibly:** Adapting thinking to different contexts and scenarios.
5. **Thinking About Thinking (Metacognition):** Awareness and control over one's cognitive processes.
6. **Striving for Accuracy:** Careful and precise thinking and actions.
7. **Questioning and Posing Problems:** Curiosity-driven inquiry and critical questioning.

8. **Applying Past Knowledge to New Situations:** Utilizing previous experiences to inform current decisions.
9. **Thinking and Communicating With Clarity and Precision:** Clear, articulate expression of ideas and thoughts.
10. **Gathering Data Through All Senses:** Comprehensive, sensory-informed learning.
11. **Creating, Imagining, Innovating:** Original and creative thinking and problem-solving.
12. **Responding With Wonderment and Awe:** Engaging with learning with enthusiasm and curiosity.
13. **Taking Responsible Risks:** Courageously trying new things despite uncertainty.
14. **Finding Humor:** Using humor to enhance resilience and community.
15. **Thinking Interdependently:** Collaborative thinking and group problem-solving.
16. **Remaining Open to Continuous Learning:** Ongoing curiosity and openness to new experiences.

Practical Strategies and Prompts for Deeper Engagement

Costa and Kallick (2008) emphasize that the Habits of Mind must be explicitly taught, modeled, and meaningfully integrated into content instruction rather than treated as isolated skills. This intentionality positions the teacher as a guide in cultivating these dispositions within authentic learning contexts. Equally important is the recognition that many students already demonstrate these habits in their lives, often without having the language to name them. These habits are not foreign concepts; they are lived and modeled daily within families and communities. It is essential to avoid deficit thinking and instead build on the strengths students already possess. With that in mind, the following strategies and reflective prompts are designed to help students intentionally apply the Habits of Mind during times of challenge, stress, or uncertainty, moments when metacognitive awareness is most needed to foster agency.

Explore *Unpacking Learner Dispositions Templates* in the Learning Tools for Clarity of Ownership appendices under the heading Co-Construction of Success Criteria and Assessment. These tools guide students in breaking down what key dispositions look like in thought, language, and action, building awareness of strengths they already use and those they want to grow.

Persisting

- **Strategy:** "Try 3 Before Me"
- **Reflective Prompts:**

    - "Have I exhausted multiple approaches before seeking help?"
    - "What strategies could I still try before deciding it's too hard?"

Managing Impulsivity
- **Strategy:** "Pause-Reflect-Act"
- **Reflective Prompts:**
  - "Am I responding thoughtfully or reacting impulsively?"
  - "What might happen if I pause and consider before speaking or acting?"

Listening With Understanding and Empathy
- **Strategy:** "Empathy Checks"
- **Reflective Prompts:**
  - "Am I actively listening, or am I merely waiting to respond?"
  - "How can I show peers I genuinely value their perspectives?"

Thinking Flexibly
- **Strategy:** "Alternate Perspectives"
- **Reflective Prompts:**
  - "How might someone else approach this differently?"
  - "What assumptions am I making that could limit my thinking?"

Thinking About Thinking (Metacognition)
- **Strategy:** "Stop-Think-Reflect"
- **Reflective Prompts:**
  - "How is my current strategy helping me achieve my goal?"
  - "What changes in my approach could improve my outcomes?"

Questioning and Posing Problems
- **Strategy:** "Inquiry Circles"
- **Reflective Prompts:**
  - "What questions do I still have that could deepen my understanding?"
  - "How might posing a new question change the direction of my learning?"

Integrating Habits of Mind Through Reflective Practices

Intentionally embedding Habits of Mind into daily reflective practices and self-assessment routines significantly deepens student ownership (Bloomberg & Pitchford, 2023; Costa & Kallick, 2008). Practical classroom strategies include the following:

- **Reflective Journaling & Metacognition:** Regular student analysis of their learning processes to identify strengths, areas for growth, and next steps.

- **Exit Tickets & Persisting:** Incorporating reflective exit tickets, prompting students to evaluate their persistence strategies and effectiveness.

- **Peer Feedback & Listening With Understanding and Empathy:** Structuring peer-assessment sessions emphasizing empathetic listening to diverse perspectives.

- **Goal-Setting Conferences & Thinking Flexibly:** Student–teacher goal-setting conferences, where learners evaluate and adjust their goals based on reflective insights, enhancing adaptability.

Check out the Learning Tools for Clarity of Ownership under the heading *Goal Setting, Self-Assessment, and Conferences* to access a ready-to-use set of *Habits of Mind Reflective Prompt Cards*. These adaptable questions help students name, apply, and transfer their Habits of Mind during daily reflection and dialogue.

Habits of Mind and Civic Empowerment

Ultimately, Habits of Mind equip students with critical civic skills, such as negotiation, advocacy, collaboration, and empathy, integral to active democratic participation (Costa & Kallick, 2008). Learners who intentionally cultivate these habits become empowered citizens, ready to engage deeply with complex societal challenges. By embedding these dispositions or habits into everyday classroom practices, educators amplify metacognitive clarity into meaningful civic empowerment, preparing students for active, reflective participation in democratic life.

Structures for Authentic, Democratic Learning Environments

Democratic ownership isn't some abstract ideal. Educators and school leaders can intentionally create structures that support it. Within such structures, educators and students share power, amplify diverse voices, and celebrate student leadership. These environments operationalize democratic values and create a tangible sense of community responsibility.

Collaboration Engages the Social Brain

 When students co-construct learning environments, they activate the brain's social cognTition systems responsible for empathy, ethical reasoning, and collective responsibility (Lieberman, 2013).

The following are examples of structures that democratize learning and promote student agency through authentic participation, reflection, and shared responsibility:

- **Reflective Practice and Restorative Circles:** Weekly structured conversations facilitate reflection, goal setting, celebration of achievements, and collaborative conflict resolution, fostering empathy, belonging, and a sense of community.

- **Student-Led Instructional Rounds:** Students engage in peer-to-peer classroom observations, analyze instructional practices, and generate evidence-based recommendations. This process democratizes instructional improvement and cultivates critical thinking, voice, and shared accountability. Chapter 8 includes a more in-depth description of Student-Led Instructional Rounds.

- **Democratic Decision-Making:** Through class voting, student-led curriculum councils, and collaboratively formed assessment committees, students actively shape their educational experiences, developing advocacy, voice, and collective responsibility.

- **Participatory Budgeting:** Students propose, discuss, and vote on how to allocate classroom or school resources, gaining real-world skills in negotiation, budgeting, and civic engagement.

- **Student-Led Conferences:** Learners take responsibility for communicating their academic progress, challenges, and goals in meetings with educators and families, building autonomy, metacognition, and a culture of transparency.

- **Youth Advisory Councils:** Representative student groups regularly collaborate with school leadership to co-create policies and initiatives, ensuring student perspectives meaningfully inform decision-making and school improvement.

- **Restorative Justice Practices:** Structures such as restorative circles or peer mediation panels center dialogue, healing, and accountability over punishment—reinforcing democratic values of fairness and communal care.

- **Youth Participatory Action Research (YPAR):** In YPAR, students act as researchers to investigate issues impacting their lives and communities. They collect and analyze data and generate action plans, engaging in a transformative process that cultivates critical consciousness, civic responsibility, and social change (Ozer, 2017; University of California, Berkeley, n.d.).

Like the aforementioned Habits of Mind, these structures and processes cultivate essential civic competencies. They empower students as active participants, preparing them for a world where their voices genuinely matter.

Check in with yourself using the *Democratic Learning Structures Checklist* and support students with the *Democratic Decision-Making Toolkit* for a more in-depth look at three ways to involve students in meaningful, collaborative decision-making. These resources are under the heading *Democratic Ownership of Classroom and Curriculum* in the Learning Tools for Clarity of Ownership.

From Shared Ownership to Civic Empowerment

The value of clarity of ownership is not limited to instructional innovation. It also equips students to engage in civic transformation. When students drive their learning through reflection, co-assessment, and goal setting, they do not just become better learners; they become better citizens. They learn the art of critical inquiry, the power of dialogue, and the responsibility inherent in decision-making.

Democratic classrooms become training grounds for life. Educators are not merely preparing students for future citizenship; they are immersing them in democracy right now, instilling lifelong habits of equity, justice, and active civic engagement.

Reflect and Act

Reflect this week: How actively do students in your classroom lead reflection, co-assessment, and goal setting? These student-centered practices flourish when paired with explicit instruction, modeling, and infusion of the Habits of Mind (Costa & Kallick, 2008).

While we ultimately aim for students to internalize and apply these habits independently, it's important to remember that ownership begins with guided exposure. As Costa and Kallick remind us, "We must allow learners multiple opportunities over time to engage with the Habits of Mind in a variety of contexts if we expect them to become habits."

Start by identifying one Habit of Mind that, if intentionally taught and practiced, could strengthen student engagement and democratic participation in your learning community. Then, commit to one deliberate next step:

- **Model student-led reflection** by explicitly teaching a habit like *Remaining Open to Continuous Learning* or *Thinking About Thinking (Metacognition)*, and invite students to analyze their learning through that lens.
- **Co-construct success criteria** with your students using habits such as *Listening With Understanding and Empathy* or *Thinking Flexibly*, making the process of assessment transparent and collaborative.
- **Facilitate goal setting** with scaffolds that encourage students to use habits like *Managing Impulsivity* or *Persisting* to set, monitor, and reflect on meaningful academic and personal goals.

Empowering students through the dual lenses of ownership and intentional habit cultivation transforms classrooms into democratic spaces where learners become reflective, responsible, and resilient contributors to their communities.

PART III:
SYSTEMS AND LEADERSHIP FOR METACOGNITIVE CLARITY

CHAPTER 8

CULTIVATING A CULTURE OF METACOGNITIVE CLARITY

Participation is not the result of learning; it is the condition for learning.
— **Carole Pateman**

Think about the most vibrant democracies—places where voices don't just coexist but actively shape decisions and outcomes. What if classrooms could function in the same powerful way, driven by the thoughtful reflections and intentional choices of learners themselves? Metacognition—this reflective practice of planning, monitoring, and evaluating one's own thinking (Flavell, 1976)—transforms students from passive recipients into active architects of their education.

In prior chapters, we stressed the need to offer students ample opportunities to practice applying metacognitive strategies to tasks and challenges. But true transformation demands more than individual practice; it calls for systemic structures and key processes or protocols that embed reflective thinking deeply into the fabric of school culture. This chapter explores five innovative structures designed to cultivate a genuine culture of metacognitive clarity:

1. Collaborative Inquiry
2. Metacognitive Equity Walks
3. Student-Led Instructional Rounds
4. Student Governance Councils
5. Youth Empowered Stewardship (YES)

Each structure shares a common thread: They call upon students to explicitly connect reflective, self-regulated, and critical thinking practices. By making cognitive processes visible and actionable, these structures foster democratic participation and empower students to lead their educational journeys intentionally and effectively.

Collaborative Inquiry for Metacognitive Clarity

What happens when educators engage in inquiry not just to improve instruction but to illuminate the thinking that drives learning? When collaborative inquiry is focused on metacognitive clarity, teams of educators work together to make the hidden processes of learning visible—both for students and for themselves. This work deepens students' capacity to plan, monitor, and evaluate their learning, while building educators' own reflective practice.

Educator teams engage in structured cycles to explore puzzles of practice: complex, recurring challenges related to student thinking and engagement. We use the term "puzzle of practice" in place of the more traditional (and deficit-laden) "problem of practice" because it hints at a stance of inquisitiveness. Rather than focusing on "right" or "wrong" answers, or "on-task" and "off-task" behaviors, a puzzle-of-practice approach centers curiosity, assets, and growth. It invites educators to investigate what students are thinking, not just what they're doing.

Collective Reflection Strengthens Insight

When educators and students reflect together, their brains engage systems that support complex problem-solving, shared meaning-making, and joint reasoning—key for collaborative learning cultures (Frith, 2012). Numerous frameworks support collaborative inquiry, but one that is particularly well-suited to cultivating metacognitive clarity is the Evidence–Analysis–Action (EAA) Framework (Bloomberg & Pitchford, 2016). This framework is

- simple and accessible, making it easy for teams to use consistently;
- asset-based, emphasizing strengths in student thinking; and
- explicitly focused on metacognitive development for both students and educators.

The Evidence–Analysis–Action (EAA) Framework

Originally developed as part of the *Leading Impact Teams Framework* (Bloomberg & Pitchford, 2017), the Evidence–Analysis–Action (EAA) cycle, depicted in Figure 8.1, is a practical and robust structure for collaborative inquiry. While it was designed to promote educator efficacy and student agency, it is especially effective when adapted to focus on students' development of metacognitive clarity.

Figure 8.1: Evidence, Analysis, Action

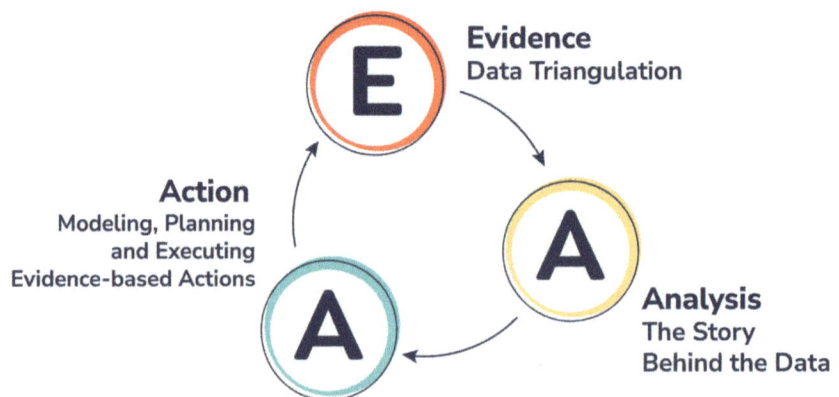

Evidence

Educators collect and examine a range of student learning artifacts, such as written responses, conversations, reflections, or performance tasks. The goal is to notice not only what students produce but how they are thinking: What strategies are they using? Where are they persisting? What assumptions or misconceptions emerge?

Analysis

Through collaborative dialogue, educators interpret the evidence to identify patterns in students' cognitive and metacognitive processes. Teams reflect on what the data reveal about how students are approaching learning and where deeper clarity or support might be needed.

Action

Impact Teams take collective action with a goal of advancing learner agency in their classrooms by intentionally analyzing evidence to determine root causes. Then, teams design intentional instructional actions anchored in self-regulation and metacognition, such as modeling specific "learning to learn" thinking strategies, co-constructing success criteria from exemplars, or embedding structured reflection and self-assessment routines to build self-awareness. They monitor the impact of these shifts on student learning and thinking, and adjust accordingly.

Review the *Metacognitive Clarity EAA Team Template* on in the Implementation and Leadership Supports under the heading *Teacher and Team Implementation Tools* for how to apply this process specifically to metacognition.

By cycling through these stages, educators develop a sharper awareness of both student and adult thinking, fostering a culture of reflection, responsiveness, and agency. Authentic collaborative inquiry expands beyond educators and students to include families, whose unique insights and capacities enhance reflective practice and metacognitive equity. Families play a pivotal role in systemic inquiry processes, reinforcing equitable outcomes through their involvement. Refer to Chapter 10 for comprehensive strategies for engaging families in collaborative inquiry.

Sample Questions to Guide Metacognitive Inquiry

To launch an inquiry, teams might begin by framing existing puzzles of practice anchored in root cause using questions that surface the "why" behind persistent challenges. These questions should move beyond surface-level symptoms to explore systemic, instructional, or learner-centered factors that may be contributing to the issue. For example, rather than asking, "Why are students scoring low on reading comprehension assessments?" a more inquiry-driven question might be, "What instructional routines or learning conditions may be impacting students' ability to transfer their understanding independently?" By rooting inquiry questions in authentic dilemmas and guided by curiosity—not blame—teams create the conditions for meaningful investigation, collective learning, and instructional transformation.

- How are our students making their thinking visible during independent tasks?
- What metacognitive strategies are students using to monitor their comprehension—and how can we tell?
- Where do students get stuck in their problem-solving, and how are they attempting to get unstuck?
- How might structured reflection opportunities deepen students' understanding of their learning processes?
- In what ways are students drawing on their cultural and community knowledge to make sense of academic tasks?

These types of questions anchor the inquiry in students' lived learning experiences while spotlighting opportunities to strengthen both instructional moves and student agency.

Impact Team Collaborative Inquiry Examples

As part of our collective effort to strengthen teaching and learning through inquiry, each team has identified key puzzles of practice grounded in student needs and instructional goals. These puzzles represent areas where we see opportunities for growth and more profound impact. Aligned with each puzzle is an inquiry question that embeds approaches anchored in self-regulation and metacognition. The inquiry questions are designed to guide team reflection, collaboration, and responsive planning to close the metacognitive equity gap. Table 8.1 captures each team's thinking and serves as an example of how inquiry can drive continuous improvement and student-centered practice across grade levels and content areas to support metacognitive clarity.

Table 8.1: Third-Grade ELA Team

PLC Puzzle of Practice	Collaborative Inquiry and Metacognitive Clarity
Students are not monitoring their comprehension well based on written responses and interviews with our students. They struggle to identify which reading comprehension strategies work best for different tasks like summarizing, identifying themes, or analyzing point of view.	How can we help students identify which reading comprehension strategies work best for them for key comprehension goals (summarizing, point of view, theme, etc.)?
Based on an analysis of student writing, it is clear that students need to work on their writer's craft. Students need more support reflecting on their writing choices and growing their writer's craft.	What learner-centered approaches can we integrate regularly to prompt self-reflection about their writer's craft approaches?
Students are not able to talk about the process they use to monitor their comprehension across subjects.	In what ways can we use close reading to explicitly model metacognitive questioning for students so they become more self-aware?
In interviewing our students who are struggling the most, they often don't realize when they've misunderstood something and don't apply strategies to fix it.	How can we support students to recognize when they misunderstand something and to proactively use strategies to clarify meaning?
When conferring with many of our students, they find it hard to explain their thinking clearly when talking or writing about texts.	What approaches can help our students articulate their thought processes clearly when responding to literature or informational texts?

Algebra Team

- What explicit routines can we implement to help students self-assess their understanding of algebraic concepts and procedures?
- How can we teach students to systematically recognize and respond to their misconceptions during problem-solving?
- In what ways can we embed opportunities for students to reflect on their solution strategies and justify their mathematical reasoning?

- How can we use formative assessments intentionally to build students' capacity for self-regulated learning in algebra?
- What instructional moves effectively guide students in evaluating the efficiency of their chosen algebraic strategies?

Physical Education (PE) Team

- How can we embed regular opportunities for students to reflect on their physical performance and personal fitness goals?
- What reflective practices can we use to help students become aware of how their effort, strategy, and teamwork impact their outcomes?
- How can we encourage students to assess and adapt their physical activities based on their own perceived strengths and areas for growth?
- What routines or tools effectively guide students to identify connections between their physical habits, wellness, and emotional well-being?
- How can we build routines for students to plan, monitor, and evaluate their progress toward achieving fitness or skill-development goals?

Seventh-Grade Next Generation Science Standards (NGSS) Science Team

- What strategies can we explicitly teach students to plan, monitor, and revise their scientific investigations for deeper understanding?
- How can we design reflective prompts or protocols that encourage students to consistently evaluate their hypotheses and evidence-based reasoning?
- In what ways can we support students in recognizing patterns of errors or misunderstandings as productive learning opportunities?
- How do structured, peer-to-peer feedback processes enhance students' ability to critically reflect on their experimental approaches and scientific explanations?
- What instructional routines most effectively build student capacity for articulating their scientific thinking and refining their conceptual models?

Social Studies (e.g., High School History Team)

- How can we regularly prompt students to reflect on how their historical perspectives shift as they engage with primary and secondary sources?
- What tools or activities help students articulate their thought processes when analyzing cause-and-effect relationships in history?
- How can we integrate opportunities for students to self-monitor their understanding of complex historical events or concepts?

- What reflective questioning routines can strengthen students' ability to critically assess their interpretations and biases about historical narratives?
- In what ways can we foster students' capacity to identify and reflect upon patterns and connections across historical themes and periods?

Kindergarten Reading Team

- How can we explicitly teach and model self-questioning strategies so our youngest learners monitor their understanding of letter sounds and early decoding skills?
- What routines or prompts can help students reflect on their strategies when blending and segmenting words?
- How do structured opportunities for self-reflection during small-group reading instruction strengthen students' awareness of successful reading strategies?
- In what ways can we encourage students to recognize when they need help understanding letters, sounds, or simple texts, and proactively seek support?
- How can we use visual cues, manipulatives, and think-alouds to help kindergarteners articulate their thinking clearly while engaging in phonemic awareness and phonics activities?

Metacognitive Equity Walks

Maya Angelou tells us that, "You find the path by walking it."

Imagine walking through not only the physical layout of a school but through its cognitive culture: the beliefs, routines, and relationships that shape how students think about their learning—and themselves.

Metacognitive equity refers to the imperative that *all* students—not just those with social capital or access to academic privilege—learn how to learn. As Dr. Saundra Yancy McGuire explains, metacognitive equity is about closing the gap between students who know how to use metacognition and those who do not and this gap frequently mirrors racial, linguistic, and socioeconomic inequities that persist in education (McGuire, 2015). These disparities are compounded when educators unconsciously hold fixed mindsets about students' intellectual capacity, or when schools fail to explicitly teach the strategies that lead to academic ownership and resilience.

Metacognitive equity walks extend the lens of traditional equity walks by centering this question: *Who is being positioned and supported as a metacognitive thinker—and who is not?* The goal is not only to examine what is taught but also to interrogate the learning conditions and expectations that either cultivate or constrain metacognitive growth, particularly for historically marginalized students.

As Impact Teams or other educator teams conduct these walks, they should do the following:

- **Engage students directly** with reflective prompts such as, "How did you approach this task?" or "What helped you when you got stuck?"—gauging whether students have access to and ownership of metacognitive strategies.
- **Scan classroom environments** for identity-affirming cues—such as multilingual scaffolds, student-authored goal-setting displays, or visual supports that guide thinking routines—looking for signs that all students are seen as capable of deep reflection.
- **Observe instruction** to assess whether metacognitive strategies are taught explicitly and equitably. Who is invited to set goals, reflect on mistakes, or self-assess? Are these practices distributed fairly, or are they reserved for students already perceived as high achievers?
- **Reflect on their own biases and assumptions**, especially around which students are "ready" for independent thinking. Research shows that educators' implicit beliefs, when left unexamined, can reproduce inequities in access to cognitively demanding tasks and learning-to-learn strategies (McGuire, 2021).

This walk becomes an equity practice when it moves beyond surface-level access to challenge deeper, structural questions: Are all students being taught to reflect, plan, and adjust their learning in ways that affirm their cultural knowledge and lived experience? Or are some students unintentionally excluded from the thinking work that cultivates self-efficacy?

The following guidance and the examples in Figure 8.2: EAA Evidence Walk Template are designed to help you envision and then implement this practice in your school(s).

Planning

Plan equity walks with clear, equity-focused prompts that invite observers to examine how teacher expectations, instructional practices, and learning conditions impact different student groups. Include guiding questions that prompt reflection on patterns of inclusion, exclusion, and unconscious bias.

Student Voice Probes (aligned to identity, equity, and metacognitive awareness):

- "What strategies are you thinking about using for this task, and how do they reflect your strengths or learning preferences?"
- "How will you know if the strategies you chose are helping you, and do you feel supported in adjusting them if needed?"
- "Have you noticed whether you get the same opportunities to share your thinking as others in the class? How does that feel?"
- "Do you think your ideas or ways of learning are understood and valued here?"

Observational Criteria (aligned to equitable and inclusive metacognitive teaching):

- Evidence that learning intentions and success criteria are co-constructed or presented in ways that are culturally and linguistically accessible to all students.

- Instructional routines that support all students—especially multilingual learners and those from historically marginalized groups—in planning their learning and articulating their thinking processes.
- Visible strategies or teacher actions that ensure equitable distribution of teacher attention, questioning, and opportunities for participation.
- Structures in place for students to reflect on their learning and experiences in ways that honor their identities and challenge deficit-based narratives.

Monitoring

Monitoring personal assumptions and biases during observations involves intentionally reflecting on how one's positionality and prior beliefs may shape interpretations of classroom interactions. This includes identifying implicit biases related to race, language, gender, or perceived ability that influence perceptions of student behavior and engagement. For example, an observer might unconsciously assume that multilingual learners are less capable and interpret their silence as disengagement rather than thoughtful processing. Or, they may notice a teacher consistently calling on White or Asian students while overlooking Black, Indigenous, or Latinx students when posing higher-order questions—an inequitable practice often rooted in unconscious diminished expectations. By critically interrogating these patterns and questioning how adult perspectives impact judgments, observers can better distinguish between equitable instructional moves and those that reinforce exclusion or marginalization.

Student Voice Probes (aligned to equity and bias awareness):

- "How do you think your background, identity, or family life shapes the way you learn or participate?"
- "Have you ever felt like your ideas were overlooked or assumed to be incorrect? What made you feel that way?"
- "When you're unsure or confused, how do you decide whether or not to speak up—and what makes that easier or harder?"
- "Do you feel like your strengths and ways of thinking are recognized in this class? Why or why not?"

Observational Criteria (aligned to equitable teaching and reflective practice):

- Teaching moves that deliberately include all students in cognitively rich tasks, especially those whose voices are often marginalized.
- Instructional practices that affirm student identity and promote culturally responsive engagement (e.g., multilingual scaffolds, diverse representations in content).
- Evidence that students are encouraged and supported to reflect on their own learning strategies in ways that acknowledge diverse strengths and cultural ways of knowing.
- Equitable questioning patterns—teachers consistently distribute higher-order questions across all student groups, regardless of perceived ability or background.

Evaluating

Evaluating the presence or absence of explicit reflective practices includes not only observing for metacognitive clarity but also examining whether all students—especially those from marginalized groups—are empowered to reflect on and make sense of their learning in ways that affirm their identities and disrupt inequitable narratives.

Student Voice Probes (centered on identity, equity, and reflection):

- "What did you notice about your thinking today that helped you feel confident or seen?"
- "How did reflecting on your work help you understand yourself as a learner?"
- "Did you feel like your ideas or strategies were valued in today's lesson? Why or why not?"
- "What helped you feel safe to take risks or share your thinking today?"

Observational Criteria (for Equitable Reflective Practices):

- Consistent use of reflective questioning that prompts students to explore not just *what* they learned, but *how* and *why*—including what influences their thinking (e.g., identity, experience, cultural background).
- Structures that support all students, especially those underrepresented or underserved, in evaluating their processes, not just their outcomes.
- Educators model vulnerability, acknowledging their own thinking and learning to foster psychologically safe spaces.
- Reflection is embedded in ways that allow for multiple modes of expression (e.g., visual, oral, multilingual).

Adjusting School-Wide Practices

Educators who commit to cognitive equity continually make adjustments to school-wide practices that provide all learners with access to metacognitive clarity. When they observe disaggregated patterns with respect to which groups of students are afforded such access, they can more effectively target their action planning.

Observational Criteria (for Equity-Centered Action Planning):

- Coherent and consistent use of inclusive, metacognitive instructional moves across classrooms—such as varied questioning strategies, multilingual scaffolds, and routines that affirm diverse learner identities.
- Observable evidence that school teams are analyzing data (including observation, voice, and disaggregated achievement) to uncover and disrupt inequitable patterns.

- Professional learning is targeted and responsive, informed by student experiences and classroom observations—especially in areas such as bias interruption, culturally responsive pedagogy, and learner agency.
- School-wide commitments to reflection and equity are visible in shared language, planning protocols, and learning design.

Examples in Action

- Impact Teams tour classrooms intentionally guided by reflective equity prompts, using observational checklists to document room environment, teaching moves, and student learning experiences.
- Participants engage in structured debriefs utilizing the EAA protocol, synthesizing observations and student conversations to uncover areas of strength and opportunities for growth.
- Action plans are collaboratively developed based on evidence gathered, explicitly targeting improvements to promote equitable, metacognitive-rich practices across the school.

Table 8.2: EAA Evidence Walk Template

EVIDENCE Observable Data on Metacognition	ANALYSIS Identify Strengths and Opportunities	ACTION Decide Next Steps
Purpose: *Why does this learning matter?* **Look-Fors:** Learning targets visible, connected to identity/justice. **Listen-Fors:** Students explain purpose ("This helps me . . .").	**Strengths:** Students articulate why learning matters. **Opportunities:** Some students are not connecting purpose to real life.	**Action Step:** Add reflection prompts ("Why is this important to me/us?") into daily practice.
Process: *How do students plan, monitor, and evaluate?* **Look-Fors:** Use of rubrics, journals, prompts, and strategy talk. **Listen-Fors:** Students describing choices, giving feedback, adjusting.	**Strengths:** Evidence of monitoring with tools. **Opportunities:** Limited peer-to-peer strategy sharing.	**Action Step:** Introduce peer reflection circles to share strategies mid-task.
Ownership: *Who drives the learning?* Look-Fors: Student goal setting, choice, and revisions. Listen-Fors: "I decided . . ."; "My goal is . . ."; "Next time I'll . . ."	**Strengths:** Some students are revising work after feedback. **Opportunities:** Goal setting is mainly teacher-directed.	**Action Step:** Co-construct success criteria and shift goal-setting to students.
Equity & Access: *Who is included and affirmed?* **Look-Fors:** All learners engaged, support for MLLs, multiple voices. **Listen-Fors:** Inclusive, affirming talk; multilingual contributions.	**Strengths:** Multiple voices represented. **Opportunities:** Limited scaffolds for language learners.	**Action Step:** Add multilingual sentence stems and equity checks into peer feedback.

Student-Led Instructional Rounds

Imagine flipping the script on traditional classroom observations: instead of adults evaluating student learning, students themselves thoughtfully and critically assess teaching practices. Picture students entering classrooms not as passive recipients but as empowered observers, thoughtfully applying clearly defined criteria to evaluate teaching effectiveness. In their groundbreaking book *Student-Led Rounds*, Joanne Buckheit and Paul Bloomberg illustrate this transformative approach, positioning students as active leaders who utilize metacognition to deeply reflect on and influence instructional methods. Review the seven steps of this process in Figure 8.1. This powerful shift exemplifies democratic education, creating classrooms where student perspectives don't just matter—they drive instructional improvement and meaningful learning experiences.

Figure 8.2: Student-Led Instructional Rounds Cycle

STUDENT-LED INSTRUCTIONAL ROUNDS CYCLE

Step 1: Select Student Participants

Step 2: Conduct Initial Briefing

Step 3: Co-Construct "Look-Fors"

Step 4: Facilitate Classroom Observations

Step 5: Prepare for Debriefing

Step 6: Conduct EAA Protocol Debrief

Step 7: Check In

Student-Led Instructional Rounds in Action

In this video, middle school students at the Michael J. Petrides School in Staten Island join their leadership team to conduct student-led instructional rounds. As they observe classrooms, students reflect on evidence from formative assessment practices and share their insights. By analyzing teaching and learning together with adults, students practice metacognition on a systems level—making their observations, reasoning, and feedback explicit. This process transforms them from passive learners into democratic partners in shaping school-wide improvement.

Planning

Through student-led instructional rounds, learners engage in metacognitively rich practices across every stage of the observation process. At the planning stage, students co-construct clear, specific criteria for effective teaching, often using rubrics or look-fors grounded in their lived experiences and learning needs. This process draws on metacognitive strategies like *chunking the task* (e.g., first identifying one key domain like student engagement before moving on to others), *analyzing exemplar videos or classroom transcripts*, and *asking self-questions* such as, "What does equitable teaching look like in action?"

Monitoring

During observations, students employ *self-monitoring* by documenting both what they notice and how they interpret it, pausing to question assumptions and identify potential biases. Strategies such as *perspective-taking, annotated note-taking templates*, and *thinking aloud* as a group support collective awareness and objective judgment.

Evaluating

In the evaluation phase, students participate in structured dialogue circles to reflect on their insights. Here, metacognitive practices such as *synthesizing evidence, evaluating consistency in their interpretations*, and *comparing judgments across observers* deepen their analytical thinking and respect for diverse perspectives.

Finally, the evaluation phase includes an adjustment stage in which students and educators engage in collaborative problem-solving to revise instructional practices. By using *goal-setting protocols, action planning templates*, and *reflective journaling*, they ensure that decisions are responsive to the data gathered and authentically aligned with students' aspirations and cultural assets.

This iterative cycle fosters students' metacognitive growth while transforming classrooms into communities of inquiry where learners are positioned as co-constructors of educational excellence.

Empowered Thinking Builds Agency

When students take ownership of observing and improving learning environments, they activate the brain's planning and monitoring systems and build strategic thinking and a sense of agency (Diamond, 2013).

Examples in Action:

- Students facilitate workshops to co-create detailed rubrics or observation criteria, clearly defining effective teaching from their collective perspective.
- Observational notes explicitly capture students' reflective thinking during classroom visits, documenting their metacognitive processes alongside their evaluations.
- Post-observation reflection circles empower students to openly share structured, actionable feedback with educators, fostering a culture of trust, reflection, and mutual learning.

The Power of Feedback

Why focus on feedback? Why not ask the students themselves? At Lefferts Park Elementary School (PS 112) in Brooklyn, fifth graders gather in a reflection circle to share how peer feedback shapes their learning. Their insights reveal how peer-to-peer feedback transforms the classroom into a community of learners where feedback is not just about correcting mistakes but about revision, growth, and preparing for future success.
These students from teacher Dierdre Byrnes's classroom show us that when feedback is democratized, learners take ownership of their progress and reimagine what it means to "do" school together.

Student Governance Councils

Imagine walking into a school leadership meeting and noticing something remarkable: students not just attending but actively guiding the agenda, facilitating thoughtful discussions, and making impactful decisions. Envision student representatives confidently collaborating alongside teachers, administrators, and community members, driven by their peers' insights, aspirations, and feedback. Student governance councils fundamentally shift school leadership from adult-driven structures with limited student influence into vibrant democratic communities where student voices authentically shape their educational experiences.

Student governance councils serve as powerful vehicles for cultivating metacognitive clarity among students by making the thinking behind decision-making processes explicit and transparent. Through this transformative approach, students routinely engage in intentional reflection about their thinking, assumptions, and decision-making strategies, leading to clearer understanding and stronger leadership capacities.

For instance, during initial planning meetings, council members might brainstorm initiatives such as an after-school tutoring program to address disproportionate dropout rates.

Initially enthusiastic about seniors tutoring freshmen and sophomores in math, students plan to implement affinity grouping principles. However, when monitoring the feasibility of their plan by collecting feedback from peers, council members uncover critical insights: many seniors, especially those from groups facing higher dropout rates, have after-school responsibilities like jobs or family care, limiting their participation. This discovery prompts explicit evaluation, where students reflect collaboratively on the biases and assumptions underlying their original idea.

Through this reflective insight, students thoughtfully adjust their approach, partnering with administrators to modify the school's master schedule and embed tutoring opportunities during the school day, ensuring equitable participation. This iterative process of reflection—planning, monitoring, evaluating, and adjusting—provides students with clear metacognitive pathways to deepen their understanding of effective governance and leadership practices.

Key Metacognitive Connections:

- **Planning:** Students explicitly identify their assumptions and outline the rationale behind meeting agendas and strategic initiatives, informed by collective student reflections, priorities, and identified growth areas.
- **Monitoring:** Student leaders continuously track peer feedback, carefully reflecting on the impact and practical implications of their council decisions, intentionally surfacing their cognitive processes.
- **Evaluating:** Structured reflective dialogues guide council members to articulate explicitly their learning, assess initiative effectiveness, and transparently identify strengths and areas needing further attention.
- **Adjusting:** Students systematically incorporate reflections and feedback into governance practices, making thoughtful adjustments that build clarity around effective leadership, decision-making, and transformative action.

Examples in Action:

- Student representatives lead monthly forums, explicitly shaping agendas through reflective conversations informed by student feedback and insights.
- Governance councils regularly gather and intentionally analyze peer feedback on initiatives, using metacognitive questioning to refine and clarify their decisions.
- Structured evaluations of school policies, practices, and leadership strategies are conducted transparently, with students clearly articulating their reflections to inform ongoing improvements.

Youth Empowered Stewardship (YES)

Imagine a vibrant community meeting where young people from diverse backgrounds lead confidently, collaborating side-by-side with adults as genuine equals. The Core Collaborative's Youth Empowered Stewardship (YES) program uniquely brings this vision to life by cultivating authentic intergenerational partnerships, deliberately centering the voices and agency of students, particularly those traditionally underserved or at the margins. Unlike traditional student councils, which often prioritize students with high GPAs and extensive extracurricular involvement, YES intentionally builds inclusive cadres that reflect the full spectrum of the student population, emphasizing equity and diversity as core strengths.

Youth Empowered Stewardship and Democratic Partnerships

Youth Empowered Stewardship (formerly Youth Equity Stewardship) is the only intergenerational pathway that builds authentic partnerships between students and adults. At its core, YES is democracy in action—young people and adults reflecting, listening, and leading together. In this video, learners share how YES has shaped their lives, helping them grow, shine, and contribute to their communities, while showing how equity, agency, and collective responsibility come alive when students co-create with adults.

Through reflective practices embedded deeply in the fabric of YES, students consistently enhance their self-awareness, critical thinking, and ability to navigate complex social issues. This explicit focus on reflective practice distinguishes YES, fostering profound metacognitive clarity that enables youth to articulate their learning processes, assumptions, and decisions. Collaborative inquiry structures further enrich these metacognitive experiences, empowering students and adults to jointly explore challenges, evaluate evidence critically, and co-create innovative solutions grounded explicitly in youth experiences and perspectives.

Creative Collaboration Sparks Cognitive Growth

Working across generations on real-world challenges engages brain systems that support imagination, perspective-taking, and deep community connection (Immordino-Yang, 2016).

Rooted in human-centered design principles, YES engages youth strategically in identifying genuine community needs and aspirations. Participants develop empathetic insights, prototype meaningful solutions, and iteratively refine their projects through reflective analysis and community feedback. Additionally, YES harnesses creative expression as a powerful communication vehicle, enabling students to compellingly convey their ideas, visions, and lived experiences through diverse arts-based methods, such as storytelling, visual art, performance, poetry, and multimedia presentations.

Key Metacognitive Connections:

- **Reflective Practice:** Continuous structured reflection enables students to examine their growth, challenge personal assumptions, and cultivate deep self-awareness and critical consciousness, positioning reflection as a core component of their learning and action.
- **Collaborative Inquiry With Human-Centered Design:** Students and adults engage collaboratively in rigorous analysis of real-world issues, enhancing young people's analytical and evaluative skills, thus empowering them to act thoughtfully and effectively. Youth in partnership with adults strategically employ planning, empathy-driven inquiry, and problem-solving to address authentic needs, continually refining projects through iterative reflection and responsive adjustment.
- **Creative Expression:** Students utilize arts-based methods to powerfully communicate complex ideas, blending intellect and emotion to advocate persuasively for transformative community change and equity.

Examples in Action:

- Diverse, intergenerational coalitions collaboratively lead impactful stewardship projects aimed at eliminating opportunity gaps, such as environmental justice initiatives, culturally responsive educational reforms, and community health campaigns.
- Arts-based inquiries enable youth to creatively express nuanced perspectives on equity, identity, and belonging through community performances, murals, poetry slams, and documentary filmmaking.
- Student-led advisories critically address educational inequities, collaboratively shaping culturally responsive policies and practices informed directly by youth voice and lived experience.
- Youth actively engage in advocacy through campaigns, community forums, and engagement initiatives that advance democratic change, with a particular emphasis on removing systemic barriers and opportunity gaps.

From Democratic Aspiration to Metacognitive Reality

Democracy is a practice to embody. Through student-led instructional rounds, collaborative inquiry, metacognitive equity walks, student governance councils, and Youth Empowered Stewardship, schools operationalize democratic principles by explicitly embedding metacognitive practices. These structures don't just cultivate better learners; they create empowered democratic participants capable of reflective thought, meaningful dialogue, and collective action today, shaping the democracies of tomorrow.

Reflect and Act

Reflect: How intentionally are you embedding structures that make metacognition a shared, democratic practice across your school community? Student-led rounds, collaborative inquiry, equity walks, governance councils, and Youth Empowered Stewardship each create pathways where students and adults reflect, monitor, and act together.

Act: Choose one structure that could most powerfully strengthen student agency and collective ownership in your context, and commit to a concrete next step:

- Launch or refine a student-led instructional round to elevate learner voice in improving teaching and learning.
- Engage your team in collaborative inquiry using EAA to analyze evidence of student thinking and design next moves.
- Conduct a metacognitive equity walk, focusing on who is—and isn't—supported as a reflective learner.
- Establish or strengthen a student governance council, where decision-making is transparent and reflective.
- Implement Youth Empowered Stewardship (YES) to foster authentic intergenerational partnerships that embody equity and justice.

Embedding even one of these structures can shift schools from places where reflection is an individual skill to communities where reflection is a shared civic habit—nurturing learners as thoughtful architects of their education and contributors to democracy.

CHAPTER 9

ELEVATING EDUCATOR CAPACITY: PROFESSIONAL LEARNING FOR METACOGNITIVE IMPACT

*Education does not change the world.
Education changes people. People change the world.*
— Paulo Freire

Take a moment to reflect on your own experience as a learner in K–12 schools. Chances are that you can remember teachers who sparked your enthusiasm to learn and even inspired you. Next, consider how often you encountered these teachers across your K–12 lifespan. While every teacher draws from their unique strengths, styles, and methods, imagine what it would be like if *every* classroom you entered as a student was a space of motivation that fueled your enthusiasm to learn. It would be a space where your own strengths, identities, and voice were affirmed. It would also be a place in which you were given the tools to not only meet academic challenges but those that impact society at large.

From Pockets of Excellence to Systems of Impact

School reform experts have often used the term "pockets of excellence" to describe classrooms or schools that demonstrate promising teaching and learning practices that exist within larger systems in which such practices have yet to be normalized. While such pockets of excellence can be found in just about any school, a common question for both researchers and practitioners is how we scale up the promising practices that show up in these isolated pockets and make them the norm across an entire school or school system.

Scaling metacognitive clarity across a school isn't simply about innovative techniques or isolated practices; it's fundamentally about creating a *culture* rooted deeply in democratic principles. If you think this sounds ambitious, you're right: We would go so far as to call it a *paradigm shift* that challenges educators to replace long-held beliefs and established practices with new ways of teaching and being. This is unlikely to happen as a result of attending a two-hour workshop, following a checklist, or (alas) even reading this book.

We won't sugarcoat the magnitude of the challenge: old habits die hard and despite a plethora of evidence that supports students taking a more active role in orchestrating their learning, most of today's schools stubbornly adhere to the traditional belief that a teacher must be a "sage on the stage," feeding kernels of wisdom to hungry (and passive) learners. The good news is that educators themselves are exceptional learners and, when given the appropriate support to engage in high-quality professional learning, they come closer to implementing metacognitive clarity in every classroom, every school. This chapter provides an overview of an evidence-based, high-impact approach to professional learning that has been used with great success by schools and districts across the country.

Why Standards-Based Professional Learning Matters

The *Leading Impact Teams Collaborative Inquiry Model*, articulated by Paul Bloomberg and Barb Pitchford (2023), aligns seamlessly with the Learning Forward Professional Learning standards, providing educators with a structured yet adaptable pathway to integrate metacognitive clarity deeply and meaningfully into educational settings. Rooted in human-centered design and collaborative inquiry, the model actively elevates the experiences, insights, and voices of students and educators alike. This intentional approach cultivates a culture characterized by meaningful reflection, learner agency, and systemic coherence—crucial elements in advancing educational equity and transformative practice.

To transition from isolated pockets of excellence to systemic transformation, professional learning must be intentionally designed. Learning Forward (2022) offers a research-based framework to ensure such transformation. Their three professional learning standards—Rigorous Content for Each Learner, Transformational Processes, and Conditions for Success—are essential to creating environments where both students and educators thrive. These standards serve as the architecture of sustainable professional learning.

1. **Rigorous Content for Each Learner:** Professional learning must be firmly anchored in robust, relevant adult learning content directly linked to improved student outcomes. When the outcome is consistent use of metacognitive practices by students, the professional learning outcomes are an educator's deep understanding of metacognitive processes and strategies, and the requisite content expertise to facilitate students' effective use of self-regulation, goal setting, and reflective practices.

2. **Transformational Processes:** The methodologies employed in professional learning significantly influence its impact. Educators must engage in collaborative, reflective, sustained, and evidence-driven processes to sustain meaningful shifts in their knowledge, skills, practices, and mindsets. Methods such as collaborative inquiry, structured reflection cycles, and Evidence-Analysis-Action protocols drive continuous growth and reinforce the transformative impact of metacognitive practices.

3. **Conditions for Success:** To achieve enduring, systemic shifts in practice, professional learning must be situated within a supportive context characterized by aligned leadership, enabling structures, and a collaborative culture. School leaders must cultivate environments that prioritize trust, collaboration, and a collective commitment to equity and continuous improvement. These conditions ensure professional learning efforts are supported, sustained, and scaled, fostering environments where metacognitive clarity can thrive consistently across all layers of the school community.

Collectively, these standards provide a frame for a coherent, actionable framework to strategically embed and scale metacognitive clarity throughout schools, transforming educator practices and significantly enhancing student learning outcomes.

1. Rigorous Content for Each Learner

Professional learning must be

- aligned to adult learning needs,
- anchored in content that improves student outcomes, and
- focused on metacognitive processes such as self-regulation and reflection.

Impact Teams address this by building educator capacity in

- reflective teaching strategies,
- embedding metacognition into curriculum and assessments, and.
- using data to adjust instruction and support learner identity.

Rigorous content is not just about the difficulty level of materials; it's about their relevance, cultural responsiveness, and potential to spark deeper thinking. This frame calls for adult learning that mirrors the best of student-centered instruction: engaging, personalized, and purposeful. Through the lens of metacognitive clarity, professional learning content should challenge educators to reflect on how they learn, how their students learn, and how to bridge the two with intentional design. For learning to stick, it must resonate with educators' values, build upon their experiences, and provide immediate tools to enhance student achievement.

2. Transformational Processes

Educators must engage in

- sustained, collaborative inquiry;
- cycles of reflection and evidence analysis that include reflective evidence;.
- redesigning practices based on culturally responsive feedback; and
- processes and practices that build strong partnerships with families, anchored in their assets.

Impact Teams integrate transformational processes through

- equity-centered redesigns of discipline and instruction,
- use of street data (Safir & Dugan, 2021) to surface student and family insights, and
- lesson study and peer coaching grounded in human-centered design.

These processes move beyond passive learning to active construction of knowledge through meaningful collaboration. Educators are positioned as learners who analyze, test, and adapt instructional practices in response to real-time student needs. Collaborative structures such as Evidence-Analysis-Action (EAA) cycles, metacognitive inquiry sessions, and peer coaching provide the foundation for collective problem-solving. This collaborative learning helps educators unlearn practices that may no longer serve students, while building more inclusive and equitable systems of support. Transformational processes anchor change in the lived realities of schools, making them durable and contextually relevant.

3. Conditions for Success

Transformative professional learning requires:

- aligned leadership and high expectations;
- protected time for reflection and collaboration;
- strategic use of funding, staffing, and tools; and
- ensuring families are co-learners in professional learning.

School leaders play a vital role by

- modeling curiosity and reflective leadership,
- establishing systems for feedback and resource monitoring, and
- prioritizing structures that remove barriers to equitable learning.

Even the most well-designed professional learning initiatives will falter without the necessary structural support. The conditions for success acknowledge that time, trust, and transparency are non-negotiable. Leaders champion learning by modeling vulnerability, reflecting openly, and committing to improvement alongside their staff, students, and families as co-learners. Policies must ensure regular, embedded time for collaboration that intentionally includes families in the learning loop. Resources must be equitably allocated to ensure all educators and families have access to the tools, language, and support they need to develop metacognitive clarity. By creating the conditions where educators and families can learn together, leaders transform professional learning from a compliance exercise into a sustained engine of collective growth and partnership.

Families as Co-Learners in Professional Learning

Scaling metacognitive clarity isn't only an instructional challenge; it's a systems learning challenge. If we want every learner to plan, monitor, and evaluate their thinking, our professional learning (PL) must treat families as equal partners and co-learners. That stance aligns directly with the aforementioned conditions for success—leadership alignment, enabling structures, and a collaborative culture—by making family engagement systemic, integrated, and sustained, rather than episodic. In brief, family members learn alongside educators in an equal power-sharing relationship.

Chapter 10 shows why this matters: effective family engagement is relational, asset-based, and linked to learning. It asks schools to build mutual capacity with families (e.g., the Dual Capacity-Building lens that is explored at length in Chapter 10) that shape adult interactions, so we design for trust and shared language from the start. In other words, family partnership is part of the learning itself. It shapes the content educators explore, the processes they use to improve, and the conditions that make professional learning sustainable.

- **Content.** Make metacognition itself family-facing content. Give educators turnkey routines (e.g., student self-assessment scripts, goal-setting templates) and a common, culturally responsive vocabulary for "thinking about our thinking" that travels home intact. Then, co-curate examples of how families already use and coach metacognition in daily life, naming those moves so students can transfer them back to class.

- **Process.** Build family voice into your Evidence-Analysis-Action (EAA) cycles: gather "street data" from families about when students use strategies at home, analyze patterns with staff and families together, and co-design the next classroom routine. This keeps PL grounded in lived experience and accelerates iteration on the metacognitive cycle.

- **Conditions.** Protect time and structures for partnership (e.g., student-led conferences focused on strategy use; brief family learning bursts attached to existing events). Leaders demonstrate the importance of metacognitive clarity by creating two-way digital spaces for reflection, and auditing home–school communication for strengths-based language. They also ensure equitable access by providing translators and signers for live events, as well as translations of written correspondence.

Practice moves (use next week).

- **Plan:** In PLCs, script two family questions that mirror your class routines (e.g., "What strategy did you try first? What will you try next?") and send them home with a visual cue card.

- **Monitor:** Add one family-reported evidence source to your next EAA (voice note, short survey, or student reflection captured at home).

- **Evaluate:** In the PLC, compare student work + family reflections; refine tomorrow's mini-lesson on *how* to choose strategies.

How we'll know it's working.

- Increased student use of shared metacognitive language in class and at home (portfolio and conference artifacts).

- Shift from one-way updates to two-way, learning-linked exchanges with families (PL audit notes).

- Uptick in strategy talk during student-led conferences and problem-solving at home (family prompts and transcripts).

Read Chapter 10 for frameworks and tools (e.g., Dual Capacity-Building, trust-building routines, and culturally responsive family workshops) to deepen these moves across your system.

What Are Impact Teams?

The Impact Team Model is a dynamic collaborative inquiry model grounded in human-centered design (HCD) and deeply supported by the formative assessment literature. Unlike traditional PLC models that often rely on top-down decision-making, Impact Teams position students and educators as partners—co-designers of the learning process who engage in evidence-informed cycles of reflection and action. This co-agency is the foundation of Impact Teams and is an aspect that sets it apart from other designs for professional learning.

Learn more and access free resources
by visiting the *Leading Impact Teams* webpage.

Rather than treating assessment as a static endpoint, the Impact Team Model advances the understanding that assessment is a process of learning (assessment for learning). This aligns with widely recognized principles from formative assessment research, which emphasize the importance of involving students in self-assessment, co-construction of success criteria, and goal setting (Black & Wiliam, 2009; Safir & Dugan, 2021). By fostering reciprocal feedback loops and collaborative sense-making, the model ensures that learning is responsive, personalized, and equitable.

Key components set the Impact Team Model apart:

- **Human-Centered Design (HCD):** Teams engage in empathy-driven cycles of inquiry, including listening to student–family voice, co-designing practices, and prototyping solutions that reflect real student needs and experiences.
- **Teacher–Student Partnership:** Students are not passive recipients of instruction. They co-construct rubrics, analyze their own progress, and reflect on their learning in partnership with educators. This shared inquiry cultivates metacognitive clarity, motivation, and efficacy.
- **Evidence-Informed Decision-Making:** Impact Teams draw on a rich mix of qualitative and quantitative data, student work, perception data, peer feedback, and reflections to guide instruction in real time.
- **Feedback as Dialogue:** Formative feedback flows in all directions—between teacher and student, student to student, and learner to self—creating a vibrant feedback culture that accelerates learning.
- **Culturally Responsive and Asset-Based:** The model embeds Universal Design for Learning and culturally sustaining practices, ensuring that every learner's cultural identity and voice are honored as central to the learning process.

Ultimately, the Impact Team Model creates a learner-centered ecosystem where assessment becomes a democratic, ongoing conversation that nurtures learner identity, amplifies voice, and builds collective efficacy. It is not merely a structure for teacher collaboration but a research-informed, equity-focused transformation of how we teach, learn, and grow together.

Review the *Metacognitive Clarity EAA Team Template* to see how your team can work together to gather and analyze evidence of metacognition to support more successful implementation. This template is in the Implementation and Leadership Supports under the heading *Teacher and Team Implementation Tools*

An Evidence-Based Approach to Transformational PL

Over the past decade, the Impact Team Model has distinguished itself nationally as a powerful form of transformational professional learning. Anchored in collaborative inquiry, this model leverages evidence-based practices to foster sustainable change across diverse educational settings. Numerous districts and schools across the country, from Dole Middle School in Hawaii to PS 9 Elementary in New York, have successfully implemented Impact Teams with measurable results, including improved student engagement, enhanced teacher efficacy, and stronger school communities (Bloomberg et al., 2023).

National Results That Inspire: The Power of Impact Teams

Over the past decade, the Impact Team Model has emerged as a national force for transformational professional learning that delivers results where it matters most: in the classroom. Rooted in collaborative inquiry and fueled by evidence-based practice, this model both inspires and sustains change.

From coast to coast, schools and districts implementing Impact Teams are seeing measurable gains in student achievement, teacher efficacy, and school-wide coherence. This isn't theory; it's practice in motion, with tangible outcomes:

- **PS 9 Naples Street Elementary (Staten Island, New York):** With a two-year focus on the metacognitive cycle, PS 9 has embedded student reflection, goal setting, and academic ownership into daily learning. The result? Over 90% of students are now meeting or exceeding achievement benchmarks, proving that when students know how to learn, they thrive.
- **Kamehameha Maui:** Māhele Lalo (Lower Division, K–5) launched learner identity cycles, where they interviewed learners regarding their learner identity. They used the Impact Team EAA framework to determine strengths and opportunities to cultivate a stronger learner identity in their students. Their plan is to build this into the goal-setting process with their students.

- **Elgin Jr./Sr. High School (Oregon):** Through structured self- and peer-assessment practices, students have gained greater autonomy and clarity. This shift has redefined engagement, not as compliance, but as ownership.
- **PS 16 (Staten Island, New York):** PS 16 increased reading proficiency dramatically by ensuring that metacognition was embedded into MTSS Tier 2 Support. Students were clear about their goals and reflected on their goals often during inquiry cycles using a standard treatment protocol to build mastery. Even though they were forced to adopt a new curriculum, they did not stop their work on building metacognitive clarity with learners; they actually refined it!
- **Sanford B. Dole Middle School (Hawaii):** Impact Teams are the heartbeat of the school's strategy to connect learners to priority standards to support mastery education. As a result, students are setting goals, tracking their progress, and making deliberate gains, especially those who have historically been marginalized. The school has been improving over the past three years.
- **Michael J. Petrides School (New York):** This K–12 complex has achieved greater staff coherence and instructional consistency through Impact Teams, resulting in elevated collective efficacy and stronger learning cultures through self- and peer-assessment practices and goal setting.

Each of these examples demonstrates the model's unique ability to foster powerful shifts in teaching and learning grounded in metacognitive clarity and driven by educator and student voice. When professional learning is done *with* teachers instead of *to* them, when students are invited to think about their thinking, and when systems align around purposeful inquiry, transformation is not only possible, it's inevitable. That's the promise of the Impact Team Model.

Scaling Metacognitive Clarity

Impact Teams provide an ideal professional learning model for scaling metacognitive clarity due to their explicit focus on teacher and student agency and reflective practice. Metacognitive clarity—understanding one's learning process and intentionally managing it—is central to developing lifelong, autonomous learners.

In the Impact Team Model, teachers are empowered as agents of change through collaborative analysis and reflective inquiry. They co-create success criteria with students, gather and analyze learning evidence, and make informed instructional decisions. This process inherently develops teachers' metacognitive abilities, empowering them to model these strategies effectively for their students.

Metacognitive Reflection for Teacher Teams and *Metacognitive Reflection for Solo Teachers*, found in the Implementation and Leadership Supports under the heading *Teacher and Team Implementation Tools*, provide structure and guidance to teachers as they reflect on what is working and determine their next steps. asfdasdfasdfasdf

Similarly, students become active participants in their own learning journey, engaging deeply in self-assessment, goal setting, and reflective practices. This dual focus on teacher and student agency builds an ecosystem where metacognitive clarity becomes normalized, consistently practiced, and explicitly taught (Bloomberg et al., 2023).

As schools scale the Impact Team approach, they cultivate a sustainable environment of ongoing inquiry, reflection, and adaptation—key conditions for embedding metacognitive clarity as a foundational element in their educational practices. The structured yet flexible nature of Impact Teams ensures that metacognitive clarity is implemented at scale and continually refined through collaborative cycles of inquiry.

Instructional Framework Alignment

To sustain metacognitive clarity beyond individual classrooms, schools need systemwide alignment. The CEL 5D+ Framework provides one lens for this alignment, making explicit connections between clarity practices and teacher evaluation. See the full alignment under the heading *Leadership and System Alignment Tools* within the Implementation and Leadership Supports. In addition, *Instructional Framework Alignment* extends this work across multiple models—including Danielson, Marzano, CUES, and others—while *Principal Evaluation Alignment* embeds metacognitive clarity in leadership standards. Together, these tools ensure that reflection and agency are scaled across the entire system.

CEL 5D+ Framework

Developed by the Center for Educational Leadership at the University of Washington, the CEL 5D+ Framework is implemented in districts across Washington, Michigan, and California. Focused on purpose, assessment, engagement, and professional collaboration, CEL 5D+ supports instructional improvement through reflection and inquiry, core tenets also found in metacognitive clarity's instructional approach.

→ **Purpose and Student Engagement**
Metacognitive clarity promotes explicit articulation of the purpose of learning and ongoing reflection, aligning seamlessly with CEL's focus on clear purpose-setting and meaningful student engagement.

→ **Assessment for Student Learning**
The Evidence-Analysis-Action cycle within metacognitive clarity aligns with CEL's formative assessment practices, emphasizing regular collection and analysis of evidence to inform instructional adjustments and student reflection.

→ **Professional Collaboration and Communication**
Metacognitive practices foster collaborative inquiry, shared professional learning, and reflective dialogue among educators, aligning directly with CEL's professional collaboration domain.

Cultivating Democratic Agency

Transforming schools into vibrant spaces of metacognitive clarity is fundamentally rooted in cultivating democratic agency, a condition wherein educators and students actively shape their educational experiences through reflective practice and collaborative inquiry. This vision, driven by the Leading Impact Teams Model (Bloomberg & Pitchford, 2023), aligns seamlessly with Learning Forward's rigorous standards for professional learning, ensuring that educators and learners alike are empowered to take meaningful, reflective action that advances educational equity and systemic transformation (Learning Forward, 2022).

At its core, cultivating democratic agency entails moving beyond isolated pockets of excellence to systemic change, where reflective practices become the norm (Hargreaves & Fullan, 2012). To achieve this, professional learning must thoughtfully integrate the standards outlined by Learning Forward, which include rigorous content, transformational processes, and conditions for success and sustainability (Learning Forward, 2022). By engaging educators deeply with rigorous, relevant content that enhances their expertise in metacognitive processes and evidence-based instructional strategies, schools lay the foundation for systemic transformation (Zelazo & Lyons, 2012). Educators equipped with this knowledge foster classrooms that actively affirm students' identities, voices, and strengths, positioning students not as passive recipients but as active participants and architects of their own learning (Bloomberg & Pitchford, 2023).

Learning Forward Standards for Professional Learning:

For more details, review the Learning Forward Standards for Professional Learning.

The transformational processes outlined by Learning Forward, such as collaborative inquiry and structured cycles of evidence-analysis-action (EAA), further solidify this democratic vision (Donohoo, 2013; Learning Forward, 2022). Through intentional, reflective dialogues and iterative problem-solving cycles, educators continuously refine their practices and mindsets, directly addressing systemic inequities and ensuring that all students thrive (Powell, 2019; Safir & Dugan, 2021). The Impact Team Model explicitly embeds democratic values of transparency, collaboration, and shared accountability, fostering an inclusive community where professional learning is shaped directly by educators' authentic needs and students' lived experiences (Bloomberg & Pitchford, 2023).

However, for democratic agency to flourish sustainably, supportive conditions must be intentionally cultivated by aligned leadership and enabling structures (Grissom et al., 2021; Jensen et al., 2016). School leaders play a pivotal role in articulating and consistently modeling a clear, compelling democratic vision that integrates reflective practice at all levels of decision-making and instructional delivery (Leithwood, 1992; Psencik et al., 2020). By strategically allocating resources, time, funding, personnel, and technology to support regular, meaningful reflection and collaboration, leaders ensure that professional learning remains deeply embedded, impactful, and equitable (Darling-Hammond, 2019; Killion, 2023).

When we cultivate democratic agency through the deliberate integration of rigorous content, transformational processes, and supportive conditions, we can transform isolated pockets of excellence into coherent, systemic practice (Learning Forward, 2022). This powerful alignment creates resilient educational ecosystems characterized by active participation, reflective dialogue, and sustained, collective action. Such an ecosystem not only enhances educator capacity and student outcomes but also cultivates learners capable of thoughtfully and actively contributing to society. In doing so, schools do more than teach; they transform, empowering individuals who are prepared to change the world (Freire, 1970).

Reflect and Act

Reflect: How intentionally does your system's professional learning cultivate metacognitive clarity—not just for students, but for educators and families as co-learners? Use Learning Forward's three standards as a lens to assess your current practice and identify where metacognitive growth is thriving and where it is inconsistent.

Act: Choose one area and commit to a deliberate next step:

- **Rigorous Content for Each Learner**
  Anchor adult learning in metacognitive practices (self-regulation, goal setting, reflection) directly tied to student outcomes.

  - *Action step:* Strengthen regular use of Evidence-Analysis-Action (EAA) protocols in PLCs to keep the focus on student thinking.

- **Transformational Processes**
  Structure collaborative inquiry around the metacognitive cycle (Plan → Monitor → Evaluate).

  - *Action step:* Launch a Metacognitive Inquiry Session in your PLC or Instructional Leadership Team (ILT), analyzing student voice and artifacts for evidence of reflection and strategy use.

- **Conditions for Success**
  Build organizational structures that protect time, equity, and access to reflective growth.

  - *Action step:* Schedule job-embedded coaching and evidence walks that surface how instructional decisions support learner thinking, ensuring all educators participate.

By aligning your system to both Learning Forward's standards and the Metacognitive Cycle, you lay the foundation for transformative, human-centered learning. This approach positions educators and their students not just as recipients of information but as self-aware learners capable of driving their own growth.

CHAPTER 10

AMPLIFYING METACOGNITIVE CLARITY THROUGH FAMILY–SCHOOL PARTNERSHIPS

In Africa, there is a concept known as "ubuntu"—the profound sense that we are human only through the humanity of others; that if we are to accomplish anything in this world it will in equal measure be due to the work and achievement of others.
— **Nelson Mandela**

When families are truly engaged as equal partners in their children's education, they're positioned to support metacognitive development in ways that complement and extend what happens in school. Engaged families help children reflect on how they learn at home, ask questions that build self-awareness about strategies, and model metacognitive behaviors in everyday life.

The difference between family involvement and engagement matters. Family involvement often means showing up for predetermined school activities. Family engagement involves co-designed and shared decision-making, where families have real input and their knowledge shapes practice. Dr. Karen Mapp's Dual Capacity-Building Framework (unpacked later in this chapter) is influential precisely because it recognizes that both schools and families must develop skills, beliefs, and relationships to work together effectively. When schools see families as equal partners, we move away from deficit thinking toward an asset-based stance that honors cultural wealth and the deep knowledge families hold about their children—perspectives that strengthen learning outcomes.

My (St. Claire) own understanding of this shift was shaped by both my study and practice. My studies at the Harvard Graduate School of Education grounded me in Dr. Mapp's Dual Capacity-Building Framework and its call for reciprocal growth. One of Dr. Mapp's essential ideas is based on co-constructing, in this case, the idea that parents/caregivers, along with educators, all build capacity as part of a true partnership. In that course, Dr. Shadae Harris pressed us to begin engagement by learning the histories of the communities we serve. Sara Lawrence-Lightfoot, another esteemed educator at Harvard, also influenced my thinking. Her book, *The Essential Conversation: What Parents and Teachers Can Learn From Each Other,* introduced the idea of "ghosts in the classroom"—the lived experiences that quietly guide family–school interactions. Both the Dual Capacity-Building Framework and the importance of ghost conversations will be discussed later in this chapter. Together, these ideas formed my metacognitive approach to parent engagement: notice the stories at play, surface assumptions, and design intentionally for partnership. In this chapter, I connect these frameworks to metacognitive clarity to show how moving from involvement to engagement transforms how we build authentic, community-rooted partnerships—and how our students learn.

School–Family Partnerships Begin With Trust and Mutual Respect

Like most successful partnerships, those between educators and families are built on a foundation of mutual respect and trust. Such relationships aren't formed overnight, and family members from underserved communities often have good reasons to be distrustful of schools and the education system in general. Some parents and caregivers have themselves had negative experiences in their own schooling as a result of deficit assumptions held by their teachers. As parents, they may feel disenfranchised due to one-way communication with school staff, where they are only contacted when there is a "problem" with their child. When schools make little effort to make family members feel welcome or included, such feelings are all the more intensified.

Rebuilding Trust

For families with negative past experiences, schools need to acknowledge these challenges directly and demonstrate consistent change over time. This requires patient relationship-building, following through on commitments, and showing genuine interest in families' perspectives and goals for their children, by addressing the "ghosts in the classroom." The phenomenon refers to unacknowledged underlying issues and negative past experiences that create obstacles in parent–school relationships, ultimately impacting student success and leading to uncomfortable parent–teacher conferences.

Sara Lawrence-Lightfoot, in her book *The Essential Conversation*, introduced the ghosts in the classroom concept. Lawrence-Lightfoot uses this phenomenon to illustrate how parents' and teachers' dialogue is connected to their early childhood experiences, which get "rehearsed and replayed in the classrooms of their children."

The term "ghosts" alludes to how these past educational experiences "haunt" present parent–teacher interactions. When parents and teachers sit facing one another, the parents are drawn back in time, to the time when they felt small and powerless, to the specters from their past (Lawrence-Lightfoot, 2003). These emotional undercurrents significantly influence the quality of the communication, and it isn't uncommon for these relationships to become adversarial.

Lawrence-Lightfoot argues that understanding these psychological dynamics is crucial for improving parent–teacher relationships and creating more productive conversations about children's education (2003). Her central thesis is about the need for more effective communication between these two vital influences in a child's life to enhance positive student outcomes.

Lawrence-Lightfoot identifies several types of "ghosts" that haunt parent–teacher conferences:

- **Memories of Feeling Small and Powerless:** These feelings of childhood vulnerability and lack of control can resurface during parent–teacher conferences.
- **Past Student–Teacher Relationship Ghosts:** Lawrence-Lightfoot (2003) explains that the "ghosts" of adults' own childhood school experiences often surface during parent–teacher conferences, shaping how they interpret a student's present learning and behavior. Both parents and teachers unconsciously project their own childhood school experiences onto the current situation. Bear in mind that a teacher who was well-served by the education system may have a limited understanding of why this wasn't the case for many of the parents with whom they interact.
- **Rehearsed and Replayed Childhood Experiences:** Lawrence-Lightfoot (2003) notes, "Their (parents and teachers) dialogue is to some extent related to their early childhood experiences, which get rehearsed and replayed in the classrooms of their children" (Conclusion, para. 4). These are unconscious patterns of behavior and emotional responses learned from their own educational experiences.
- **Specters From the Past:** Actions and reactions from parents and educators relate to unresolved emotional experiences from their own time as students.

The central theme is that these ghosts create barriers to effective communication because both parents and teachers are unconsciously responding not just to the present situation but to their past educational traumas, disappointments, and power dynamics from when they were children in school.

In order to eradicate these "ghosts in the classroom," families and the school must take on the role of "ghost busters." Lawrence-Lightfoot's identification of the various ghosts that haunt parent–teacher conferences reveals a profound truth about human psychology and educational relationships, a truth that the brilliant writer James Baldwin captured in *The White Man's Guilt*: "History is not the past. It is the present. We carry our history with us. We are our history. (1965)" These spectral presences from their educational histories create an invisible but powerful force that shapes every interaction, often undermining the very communication these meetings are meant to foster. Neither parents nor teachers may fully recognize how their own buried school experiences are influencing their ability to advocate for or understand the child at the center of the conference. Until educators and parents alike acknowledge and confront these ghosts from their past, parent–teacher conferences will continue to be haunted spaces where the needs of present-day children become secondary to the unresolved emotional business of the adults meant to serve them.

School leaders can play a role in helping to mitigate the damage caused by these unresolved tensions. Leadership must actively work to create welcoming environments that signal families are valued partners. This means examining current practices through families' eyes—from how phone calls home are framed (celebrating successes, not just addressing problems) to how meetings are scheduled and conducted. Schools should audit their communication practices to ensure they're accessible, culturally responsive, and strength based.

Listening Session Questions for Families and Caregivers

Before we begin, we want to acknowledge that schools are not neutral spaces. For many families, past experiences, both positive and painful, continue to shape how it feels to walk into a classroom or meet with a teacher. Even when the goal of such meetings is undeniably positive (e.g., determining how to best support the child), when past trauma is reactivated, parent–school interactions feel heavy. The questions that follow are designed to create space for honesty, healing, and partnership—so that together, we can learn from the past and build a more trusting, joyful future for your children.

1. Acknowledging Past Experiences and Harm

- Has the school ever harmed you or your child—directly or indirectly? If so, how?
- When you think back to your own experiences as a student, what feelings or memories come up when you walk into a school now?
- Do you ever feel "small" or "powerless" in interactions with educators? What might help shift that dynamic?

2. Rebuilding Trust

- What would it take for you to fully trust this school with your child's well-being and learning?
- Can you recall a time when the school followed through on a commitment or showed genuine care for your family? What made that meaningful?
- What's one step the school could take right now to repair or strengthen its relationship with you?

3. Recognizing Strengths and Joy

- What brings your child joy in learning, inside or outside of school?
- When has the school recognized your child's brilliance or unique strengths? What did that feel like for you as a parent?
- How do you want teachers to talk about your child when you're not in the room?

4. Partnership and Voice

- Do you feel your voice is heard and respected when decisions are made about your child? Why or why not?
- What would an ideal parent–teacher conference look and feel like to you?
- How can the school better partner with you to set goals for your child's future?

5. Looking Forward

- Imagine this school three years from now. What would need to change for you to feel fully welcomed, respected, and valued here?
- What does success look like for your child, not just academically, but as a whole person? How can we support that vision together?
- What message do you hope your child carries about themselves and their education when they graduate from this school?

Understanding the Dual Capacity-Building Framework

Developed by Karen Mapp and Eyal Bergman (2019), the Dual Capacity-Building Framework (Version 2) offers a strategic vision for effective family–school collaboration. Rather than providing a rigid blueprint, it identifies essential conditions, capacities, and outcomes that schools and families must develop collectively. This approach recognizes the unique contexts of diverse school communities and emphasizes family engagement as a cornerstone for equitable student achievement.

The framework identifies two primary challenges:

- Educators often lack exposure to robust examples of family engagement, may have received minimal training, or could view family partnerships through a deficit lens.
- Families might feel marginalized due to past negative experiences (the aforementioned "ghosts") or sense a general lack of respect. Too often, they are offered limited opportunities to contribute to the school community.

To effectively address these challenges, schools must intentionally establish conditions that nurture productive family–school partnerships. Mapp and Bergman described two sets of conditions that must be in place to make such partnerships possible: process and organizational.

The following process conditions highlight essential characteristics that enable schools to form meaningful, sustainable engagement with families:

- **Relational:** Built on mutual trust, crucial for meaningful partnership.
- **Linked to Learning and Development:** Engagement is directly connected to student academic and metacognitive growth.
- **Asset-Based:** Recognizing and celebrating the strengths and knowledge families bring.
- **Culturally Responsive and Respectful:** Valuing diverse family backgrounds and lived experiences.
- **Collaborative and Interactive:** Ensuring genuine two-way communication and shared decision-making.

Alongside effective process conditions, establishing robust organizational conditions is essential for meaningful family–school partnerships. These organizational factors ensure that family engagement is prioritized, systematically integrated into school culture, and consistently supported by leadership, resources, and infrastructure.

- **Systemic:** Embraced by school leadership as central to educational practice.
- **Integrated:** Embedded intentionally into all school strategies and initiatives.
- **Sustained:** Supported consistently with resources and infrastructure.

To operationalize effective family–school partnerships, schools and families must intentionally develop key capacities. The Dual Capacity-Building Framework identifies four critical areas known as the "4 Cs," essential for deepening collaboration, fostering mutual understanding, and ensuring sustainable, transformative family engagement practice. Central to the Dual Capacity-Building Framework is the goal of building capacity in four critical areas:

- **Capabilities:** Enhancing the skills and knowledge needed for effective family–school collaboration through intentional skill development, shared understanding, and ongoing communication between all stakeholders in a child's educational journey.
- **Connections:** Building supportive networks among families and educators. Examples include mentoring programs in which experienced families who have engaged in successful partnerships mentor those who are new to the program. Another example is multilingual parent liaisons, who help bridge communication gaps.
- **Cognition:** Shifting beliefs and values toward seeing families as essential partners. This can be accomplished with focused professional development, including home visits and storytelling sessions in which families share their cultural backgrounds and educational values with staff. Most importantly, family–school partnerships should never be relegated to one-shot workshops but instead require comprehensive, job-embedded professional learning.
- **Confidence:** Strengthening self-efficacy in both families and educators, empowering shared leadership.

Families as Natural Metacognitive Experts

As we have emphasized, effective partnerships are built on mutual trust and respect. It therefore stands to reason that educators should strive to identify and acknowledge the many assets of the families with whom they partner. One of the most overlooked truths in teaching and learning is that families already have deep expertise in metacognition, although they may not call it that. Every day, in ways both intentional and instinctive, families guide children to think about their thinking, plan ahead, monitor progress, and adjust course. These are the very habits that define metacognitive clarity.

Families possess this expertise because metacognition is not solely an academic skill; it is a life skill rooted in lived experience. Parents and caregivers use it to manage households, balance work and responsibilities, budget time and resources, and solve problems in real time. They continuously model self-awareness ("What's working?"), self-monitoring ("Do we need to adjust?"), and self-regulation ("How do we respond?") in ways children absorb long before they hear the term *metacognition* in school.

When schools and families intentionally partner to build metacognitive clarity, the results multiply. Schools bring structured frameworks, shared language, and intentional practice across subject areas. Families bring cultural wisdom, lived experience, and authentic contexts where metacognitive strategies are applied in everyday life. Together, they create a seamless web of support where students not only learn *what* to think but *how* to think about their thinking at school, at home, and in the community.

Three Everyday Examples of Family Metacognitive Expertise

1. Daily Routines: Planning and Anticipating Needs

    The night before an important day, a parent double-checks the weather, makes sure the clean clothes are ready, and talks with their child about the morning's schedule. They remind the child to pack lunch and put it by the door so nothing is forgotten in the rush. Here, the parent is guiding the child through *planning ahead, anticipating obstacles,* and *creating environmental cues*—all core metacognitive strategies.

2. Problem-Solving: Adapting When Plans Change

    Dinner is cooking, but halfway through, they realize a key ingredient is missing. Rather than abandoning the meal, the family brainstorms substitutions using what they have on hand. The child is invited into the conversation: *What could we use instead? How will that change the taste?* This is real-time *flexible thinking, monitoring progress toward a goal,* and *evaluating options.*

3. Cultural Traditions: Transferring Knowledge Across Contexts

    During a family gathering, an elder teaches a traditional game or recipe, explaining each step and why it matters. The child not only learns the process but also hears strategies for remembering tricky parts, like rhymes, stories, or physical cues. Later, the child uses the same memory tricks to recall steps for a science project at school. This is *knowledge transfer* and *strategic memory use*, both hallmarks of metacognition.

Advancing Metacognitive Clarity With Families

Rather than traditional models where families are asked to help with predetermined activities, schools should consider creating genuine opportunities for families to contribute their expertise and perspectives. This might include involving families in curriculum planning, school improvement decisions, or having them share their professional skills and cultural knowledge with students. The key is moving from "helping the school" to "shaping the school together." This creates a strong sense of belonging and ownership for families, strengthening relationships within the school ecosystem.

If we want families to become active partners in building metacognitive clarity, we must first help them *name* and *claim* the expertise they already hold. Since many parents and caregivers already use sophisticated metacognitive strategies daily without realizing they are doing so, we can collaborate with them to make these strategies visible through shared language, concrete examples, and collaborative reflection. In this way, we empower families to see themselves not as supporters of learning but as co-architects of it.

How to Build Meaningful Partnerships

- **Start with storytelling.** Invite families to share everyday moments where they've helped their child plan ahead, solve a problem, or adjust after a setback. Listen for the metacognitive strategies embedded in those stories and reflect them back in plain language.
- **Create a shared vocabulary.** Offer simple, culturally responsive terms for metacognitive practices, such as *"thinking about your thinking"* or *"planning your next move,"* so families can use the same language at home that students hear in school.
- **Connect home to school.** Show families how the same skills they nurture—like breaking tasks into steps or rethinking an approach—are also essential in academic contexts.
- **Celebrate their role.** Acknowledge that families are already teaching their children these skills in authentic, meaningful contexts. This builds confidence and reinforces that their contribution is essential to the school's vision.

When families recognize that they are already skilled metacognitive coaches, they can speak about their role with pride, intentionally model these strategies, and join educators in creating a culture of metacognitive clarity that spans home, school, and community.

Reflective Questions for Families

These questions can be offered during a family workshop, printed in a school newsletter, or shared in one-on-one conversations:

- When was the last time you helped your child plan ahead for something important? How did you do it?
- How do you encourage your child to keep going when something feels hard?
- What strategies do you use at home to help your child remember important tasks or steps?
- Can you recall a time you and your child solved a problem together? What thinking steps did you take?
- How do you help your child learn from mistakes or setbacks?

Family Partnerships That Foster Metacognitive Clarity

The most powerful partnerships are born when schools see families not as participants on the sidelines but as equal partners in shaping learning. This was the central lesson I (St. Claire) encountered in the work of Dr. Shadae Harris during my studies at Harvard Graduate School of Education—a lesson that has profoundly influenced my leadership practice. Harris, an education consultant and expert on family and community engagement, underscores the importance of honoring the "funds of knowledge" that every stakeholder brings—educators, families, and community members alike (Moll et al., 1992). When these diverse forms of expertise are recognized as equally valuable, trust grows, relationships deepen, and the conditions for advancing metacognitive clarity take root.

Harris stresses the importance of understanding the local context when identifying which community or population might be underserved, since these populations vary from place to place. Effective engagement requires educators to be well-versed in the history, demographics, and culture of the communities they serve. For metacognitive educators, this isn't simply about gathering facts—it's about reflecting on how assumptions shape interpretation and intentionally practicing self-awareness as part of the engagement process.

Based on Harris's approach, here are key ways educators can connect their methods to metacognitive practice:

- **Structured Reflection Through Community Walks**
  Use community walks as a metacognitive exercise, documenting not only what is observed but also the thought processes and biases that shape interpretation.

- **Empathy Interview Analysis**
  Conduct empathy interviews—one-on-one conversations designed to surface lived experiences—as opportunities to practice deep listening, question assumptions, and notice how preconceptions might distort understanding.

- **Communities as Learning Laboratories**
  Treat communities as spaces for educator growth, applying the metacognitive cycle to engagement:

  - *Plan:* Set learning goals about community history and context.
  - *Monitor:* Track how your understanding develops.
  - *Evaluate:* Assess the effectiveness of your engagement strategies.
  - *Adjust:* Refine your approaches based on what you discover.

- **Analyzing Local Data**
  Examine evidence of impact by looking at data (such as attendance patterns) to determine whether outreach efforts are leading to meaningful changes in family engagement.

Harris's work positions communities not as "subjects" of engagement but as co-teachers in the learning process. For educators committed to metacognitive clarity, this means every step of engagement doubles as a reflective exercise, strengthening not only relationships with families but also their own awareness of how beliefs, biases, and strategies shape practice.

Metacognitive Moves for Family Engagement (After Harris)

- **Community Walks** → Reflect on what you see *and* how your assumptions shape interpretation.
- **Empathy Interviews** → Listen deeply, notice biases, and surface family stories as knowledge.
- **Cycle Your Learning** → Plan → Monitor → Evaluate → Adjust your engagement strategies.
- **Use Local Data** → Track whether outreach efforts actually shift trust, attendance, and partnership.

These practices turn family engagement into a metacognitive exercise for educators—building trust, surfacing assumptions, and treating communities as co-teachers in the learning process.

Strategies for Integrating Metacognitive Clarity With Families

Families play a crucial role in fostering metacognitive clarity by reinforcing practices such as reflective questioning, goal setting, and self-assessment within home environments. Research demonstrates that students who are taught to use metacognitive strategies early on are more resilient and more successful, both in and out of school. Families, when engaged as genuine partners, can

- co-create success criteria and goals, reinforcing reflective thinking;
- support and monitor their children's progress, strengthening agency and ownership; and.
- encourage resilience, adaptability, and strategic thinking, aligning with essential metacognitive habits.

Schools can expand family engagement in metacognitive development through several strategic approaches:

- **Structured Communication Systems:** Schools can establish regular communication protocols that go beyond traditional progress reports. This includes sharing specific examples of metacognitive strategies being taught in class, sending home reflection prompts that families can use during homework time, and creating shared vocabulary around self-regulation and learning processes. Weekly or biweekly "metacognitive newsletters" can highlight strategies families can reinforce at home.
- **Family Learning Workshops:** Offering workshops that teach parents specific metacognitive techniques helps create consistency between school and home environments. These sessions can demonstrate how to ask effective reflective questions, such as "What strategies worked well for you today?" and "What would you do differently next time?" You can also model goal-setting conversations and provide tools for supporting self-assessment at home.
- **Digital Platforms for Collaboration:** Schools can develop or utilize platforms where families and teachers collaboratively track student progress toward metacognitive goals.

These systems allow parents to see what strategies their children are learning, provide input on home observations, and celebrate growth in self-awareness and strategic thinking together with educators.

- **Home–School Learning Contracts:** Creating formal agreements where families and schools jointly commit to specific metacognitive practices strengthens accountability. These might include agreed-upon reflection routines, shared goal-setting sessions, or consistent use of self-assessment tools across both environments.
- **Cultural Responsiveness in Metacognitive Practices:** Schools can work with families to understand how different cultural backgrounds approach reflection, goal setting, and self-assessment. This allows for adaptation of metacognitive strategies that honor family values while building universal skills in self-regulation and strategic thinking.
- **Parent–Student–Teacher Conferences:** Restructuring conferences to focus specifically on metacognitive development—where students lead discussions about their learning strategies, challenges, and goals while parents and teachers collaborate on support plans—makes families true partners in the metacognitive journey.
- **Take-Home Metacognitive Toolkits:** Providing families with concrete resources like reflection journals, goal-setting templates, and strategy cards gives them practical ways to reinforce school learning at home while maintaining consistency in approach and language.

Supporting Metacognitive Development at Home

1. Supporting and Monitoring Progress at Home
    - Learning Conversations: Parents engage in structured conversations about what students learned, how they learned it, and what they found challenging.
    - Strategy Sharing: Families learn and practice specific metacognitive strategies alongside their children.
    - Progress Monitoring Tools: Parents use school-provided checklists and rubrics to track metacognitive skill development at home.
2. Reinforcing Agency and Ownership at Home
    - Student-Led Homework Reviews: Children explain their homework process, strategies used, and areas needing improvement. (Families can also help guide these conversations with structured reflection sheets provided by the school.)
    - Choice and Voice Opportunities: Families provide options for how children demonstrate learning and reflect on their choices.
    - Self-Assessment Integration: Parents guide children through self-evaluation before reviewing work together.

Parents and caregivers can further support metacognitive development with the following moves:

- Ask process-focused questions: "How did you figure that out?" rather than "Is that right?"
- Encourage children to identify their own mistakes before offering help.

- Celebrate metacognitive growth alongside academic achievement.
- Finally, returning to our theme of collaboration and co-creation, families and schools can work together in the following ways:
1. Collaborative Strategies for Building Resilience and Strategic Thinking
   - **Strategy Toolkits:** Jointly develop metacognitive strategy cards that students can use at school and home.
   - **Growth Portfolio Systems:** Students maintain portfolios showing metacognitive development that are reviewed by both teachers and families.
2. Implementing Alignment and Communication Systems
   - **Metacognitive Learning Walks:** Parents observe classroom practices and learn how to reinforce similar approaches at home.
   - **Digital Communication Platforms:** Real-time sharing of metacognitive goals and progress between school and home.
   - **Family Metacognitive Workshops:** Regular sessions where families and educators practice metacognitive strategies and learn implementation techniques.

Moving Forward Together: Families as Co-Architects of Metacognitive Clarity

True partnership means moving from doing things *for* families to doing things *with* families. When we honor parents' lived wisdom and make their strategies visible, we erase the "ghosts in the classroom" and build trust where harm once lived. Families are not supporters of learning—they are co-architects of it. By reflecting, planning, and growing together, we model for our children the very metacognitive clarity they need to thrive—and we remind them that home, school, and community are united in their brilliance.

To make these strategies more accessible, we've included *Family Conversation Guide: Talking About Thinking at Home* in the Learning Tools for Clarity of Ownership. This tool helps parents and caregivers talk with their children about thinking in ways that are natural, affirming, and connected to daily routines.

Family Engagement as a Democratic Practice

Genuine family–school partnerships exemplify democratic practice. They encourage shared decision-making, elevate diverse voices, and collectively pursue equity. When families actively co-lead equity initiatives, schools become vibrant centers of democracy, characterized by mutual respect and collective efficacy. Here are some examples:

- **Community Equity Teams:** Families, students, and educators co-analyze a range of school-wide data, including screeners, diagnostics, climate and perception data, and evidence collected during instructional rounds to build a culture of metacognitive clarity. They set shared learning intentions and success criteria, surface assumptions, make thinking visible with claim–evidence–impact notes, and run rapid Evidence–Analysis–Action cycles to co-design and test equity-focused solutions (e.g., competency-based grading shifts, learner-centered assessment routines, and multilingual learner supports), followed by plan–monitor–evaluate reflections to track impact.

- **Family Advisory Councils:** Families build decision metacognition by co-constructing the learning intention and success criteria for each agenda item, using an equity-impact rubric and "Because . . . therefore . . ." reasoning to choose curriculum, metacognitive strategies, and policies—then closing with "I used to think / Now I think" reflections to refine future decisions.

- **Participatory Budgeting Processes:** Schools partner with families and students to co-lead budgeting committees that cultivate a culture of metacognitive clarity. Every proposal follows plan–monitor–evaluate routines: define the learning intention and success criteria (plan), make reasoning and evidence public with an equity-impact rubric (monitor), and compare predicted versus actual outcomes to inform the next cycle (evaluate), guiding allocations for materials, extracurriculars, and culturally responsive resources.

- **Culturally Affirming Events:** Families, students, and educators co-plan and lead heritage nights and storytelling circles to build a culture of metacognitive clarity, opening with a shared learning intention, embedding brief thinking routines at each station ("notice/wonder," "Because . . . therefore . . ."), and closing with "I used to think / Now I think" reflections that make reasoning visible and strengthen community pride.

Through these authentic democratic practices, family–school partnerships become dynamic engines of equity and collective empowerment, enriching educational experiences and outcomes for all students.

Overcoming Common Barriers

As we discussed at the beginning of this chapter, building effective partnerships requires intentionally addressing barriers such as historical mistrust, deficit perspectives, and communication gaps. Here are some strategies:

- **Explicit Trust-Building:** Structured relationship-building routines.
- **Asset-Based Engagement:** Consistent recognition and leveraging of family strengths.
- **Equity-Centered Practices:** Reflective dialogues around equity and inclusion, ensuring diverse perspectives are honored and included.

Amplifying metacognitive clarity through family–school partnerships is an ethical and democratic imperative. The Dual Capacity-Building Framework provides the strategic compass needed to guide meaningful engagement, creating robust conditions that enable all learners to thrive. Through intentional collaboration, mutual trust, and asset-based thinking, families and schools together cultivate resilient, reflective, and empowered communities, laying the foundation for sustained educational excellence and collective transformation.

What the Science Says

Strong family–school partnerships are not just supportive structures; they are powerful engines for developing metacognitive clarity in students. When families and schools collaborate intentionally, they create learning ecosystems where young people know how to think about their thinking, monitor their strategies, and adjust their approaches to challenges. This partnership transforms everyday interactions into opportunities for self-regulation, resilience, and academic growth.

Research indicates that effective family–school partnerships in metacognitive development lead to these outcomes:

- **Enhanced self-regulation.** Sustained, constructive parental involvement (e.g., expectations, organizing learning at home, supporting homework quality) predicts students' use of metacognitive strategies, which in turn mediate higher achievement (Veas et al., 2019).
- **Improved academic outcomes.** When schools, families, and communities coordinate around shared goals, student achievement improves across ages and backgrounds (Henderson & Mapp, 2002).
- **Increased resilience.** Metacognitive reflection—monitoring one's thinking, emotions, and strategies—supports adaptive coping and future-oriented adjustment, a core tenet of self-regulated learning models (Efklides, 2011).

The science is clear: when families and schools partner around metacognition, students gain more than mastery. They learn to regulate their learning, adapt to challenges, and persist—skills that fuel success in school and in life.

Academia Avance Charter School Case Study

The family engagement model at Academia Avance Charter School in Los Angeles exemplified a sophisticated approach that fosters multiple pathways to metacognitive clarity for students, families, and the broader educational community.

These examples illustrate practical approaches that successfully integrate family partnerships into the fabric of educational systems, deeply embedding metacognitive clarity into home–school practices.

- **Structural Elements Supporting Metacognitive Development:** Academia Avance had a strong Parent Advisory Committee (PAC). The Parent Advisory Committee's involvement in decision-making and resource allocation created a transparent feedback loop where families actively reflected on educational needs and outcomes. Through their fundraising, teachers were able to apply to the PAC for mini-grants for classroom resources. When parents provided mini-grants for field trips and learning materials, they were engaging in metacognitive processes about what learning experiences will be most beneficial.

- **Regular Reflective Practice:** Every Tuesday, families gathered for their weekly empowerment and bonding sessions. This served as a consistent opportunity for metacognitive engagement. Families were not just participating in activities; they were collaborating and attending workshops that likely involve reflection on learning processes, problem-solving strategies, and educational goals. The mental health advancement sessions led by the social worker \ supported metacognitive clarity by helping families develop awareness of their thinking patterns, emotional responses, and coping strategies. Families also engaged in arts and crafts, producing drawings and paintings, learning how to do flower arrangements, and enhancing their skillsets.

- **Student-Led Conferences as Metacognitive Catalysts:** The student-led conference model is one of the most direct connections to metacognitive clarity. Academia Avance had an attendance rate of 95% to 98% at their parent–teacher conferences. During these conferences, the students, teacher, and family set goals as a team and identify the roles that each can play in supporting their student. When students led their parent–teacher conferences, they

    - reflected on their learning progress and challenges,
    - articulated their understanding of their strengths and growth areas,
    - thought about their thinking processes and learning strategies, and
    - took ownership of goal setting and solution identification.

    This approach transformed students from passive subjects of discussion into active metacognitive agents who had to analyze and communicate their learning journey.

- **Solution-Driven Focus:** Academia Avance focused on solution-driven conferences that promote metacognitive clarity by requiring all parties—students, families, and teachers—to move beyond problem identification to strategic thinking about interventions and support systems. This required metacognitive skills like planning, monitoring, and evaluating potential approaches (Henderson & Mapp, 2002; Veas et al., 2019).

- **Community-Wide Metacognitive Culture:** The 95% to 98% conference attendance rate suggests that this metacognitive approach has become embedded in Academia Avance's school culture. Nearly all families consistently engaged in reflective, goal-setting conversations about their children's learning, and this creates a community norm of metacognitive awareness and shared responsibility for educational outcomes within the school.

Academia Avance's comprehensive engagement model transformed the entire school community into a metacognitive learning system where reflection, strategic thinking, and collaborative problem-solving became the norm rather than the exception within the school ecosystem.

Tools for Family–School Partnerships

- **Family Conversation Cards** → Simple prompts for families to ask at home (e.g., *"What strategy worked for you today?"* / *"What will you try differently tomorrow?"*).
- **Metacognitive Workshop Guide** → A turnkey outline for a 45-minute family session on goal setting, reflection routines, and self-assessment.
- **Advisory Council Protocol** → Step-by-step process for co-constructing learning intentions and success criteria with families, students, and staff.
- **Home to School Reflection Journals** → Shared journals where students, teachers, and families document strategies, challenges, and next steps.
- **Equity Impact Rubric** → A tool for advisory councils or budget committees to evaluate decisions, with prompts like *"Whose voices shaped this?"* and *"Who benefits?"*

These resources make family engagement tangible, positioning families as co-architects of metacognitive clarity. See the online appendices for reproducible templates.

Family Engagement as Collective Agency

When rooted in democratic practice, family engagement fuels equity, metacognitive growth, and collective transformation. From equity teams to student-led conferences, these partnerships move beyond involvement to authentic co-leadership. By embedding reflection, transparency, and shared responsibility, schools build resilient learning communities where students, families, and educators think together about thinking and sustain excellence through shared agency.

Reflect and Act

Reflect: Are families in your school treated as helpers on the margins—or as co-architects of learning? True partnerships honor families' lived expertise, rebuild trust where harm has existed, and recognize that families are natural metacognitive coaches.

Act: Choose one action that can deepen family–school partnership and amplify metacognitive clarity:

- **Honor lived expertise** → Invite families to share everyday strategies for planning, problem-solving, and reflection—and name them as metacognitive practices.
- **Co-design with equity** → Create advisory councils, equity teams, or budgeting processes where family voices shape decisions.
- **Embed reflection routines** → Close workshops or conferences with prompts like *"I used to think . . . Now I think . . ."* to make reasoning visible.
- **Align across contexts** → Use newsletters, digital platforms, or toolkits so home and school reinforce the same strategies.
- **Commit to one sustained shift** → Reframe a routine (e.g., conferences, family workshops) into a co-learning space—and sustain it long enough for culture to change.

When schools and families reflect, plan, and act together, metacognitive clarity becomes a shared democratic practice—strengthening agency, resilience, and belonging for every child.

CHAPTER 11

THE FUTURE OF LEARNING IS METACOGNITIVE

The real danger is not that computers will begin to think like humans, but that humans will begin to think like computers.
— **Sydney J. Harris**

When the World Economic Forum (WEF) identified critical thinking, adaptability, complex problem-solving, and self-management as cornerstone skills required by 2027, it wasn't simply outlining an educational wish list; it was sounding an urgent alarm (WEF, 2023, p. 31). The Skills Imperative 2035 (NFER, 2023, p. 8), a research endeavor that seeks to identify essential employment skills people will need for work by 2035, further underscores this urgency, projecting that creativity, resilience, teamwork, and advanced problem-solving will be indispensable for navigating future challenges driven by rapid technological advancements, shifting demographics, environmental upheavals, and the accelerating proliferation of artificial intelligence (AI).

AI-driven technologies are rapidly reshaping the workforce and societal dynamics, automating routine tasks and amplifying the importance of distinctly human competencies such as emotional intelligence, creativity, and ethical reasoning (Brynjolfsson & McAfee, 2017; WEF, 2023). As impressive as the strides in AI technology are, it simply cannot reproduce the qualities that make us human. Despite this profound transformation, educational systems frequently remain tethered to compliance-driven models emphasizing standardized testing, rote memorization, and transactional teaching methodologies that are better suited to preparing our students to work in industrial-age factory jobs that no longer exist rather than meeting the challenges of the post-AI workplace.

Additionally, AI has significant potential to exacerbate existing educational and social inequities. Algorithmic biases embedded within AI systems can unintentionally perpetuate and amplify systemic disparities, disproportionately affecting students from historically marginalized communities (Benjamin, 2019; Noble, 2018). Here are some concrete examples:

- AI-driven personalized learning platforms may inadvertently prioritize students who already exhibit strong academic performance, allocating more resources and support to advantaged students, thereby widening existing opportunity gaps (Selwyn, 2021; Warschauer & Matuchniak, 2010).

- Digital assessment tools can inaccurately evaluate multilingual learners or students from diverse cultural backgrounds by mislabeling linguistic differences as deficiencies, reinforcing inequitable assessments and outcomes (García & Kleifgen, 2018).
- Schools in economically disadvantaged communities often lack essential infrastructure, such as reliable high-speed internet and advanced computing devices necessary to effectively implement AI-enhanced educational tools, further deepening the digital divide (Warschauer & Matuchniak, 2010).
- Predictive analytics used in behavior management systems may disproportionately flag and penalize students from marginalized backgrounds due to biases present in historical disciplinary data, exacerbating systemic inequities in school discipline (Eubanks, 2018; O'Neil, 2016).

Concerns about bias also specifically apply to speech recognition technologies frequently employed in educational settings (Koenecke et al., 2020):

- **Algorithmic Bias:** Speech recognition systems often struggle to accurately recognize diverse accents, dialects, and pronunciation variations common among multilingual learners, potentially misclassifying their proficiency or skills (Blodgett et al., 2020).
- **Misinterpretation of Speech Difficulties:** Students with speech disorders or articulation challenges may be inaccurately assessed, as software may misunderstand or fail to comprehend their speech patterns, leading to potentially erroneous proficiency assessments (Koenecke et al., 2020).
- **Equity and Access Concerns:** Speech recognition systems predominantly trained using data from native or fluent English speakers inherently disadvantage multilingual learners and students experiencing speech difficulties, raising critical equity concerns (Blodgett et al., 2020; Koenecke et al., 2020).

Given these potential biases and inequities, educators advocate for vigilant monitoring and intentional safeguards to ensure equitable assessments, particularly for diverse student populations (Benjamin, 2019; García & Kleifgen, 2018). Recommended proactive measures include

- regular analysis of assessment data to identify and address disparities promptly,
- integration of human observation and professional judgment alongside AI-driven assessments, and
- provision of targeted supplementary support for students identified as multilingual learners or those experiencing speech-related challenges, ensuring equitable educational opportunities and outcomes.

Ethical Guardrails for AI in Classrooms

Checklist for educators and leaders:
- Ensure human judgment supplements AI-driven assessments.
- Monitor disaggregated data for algorithmic bias.
- Provide equitable infrastructure (devices, internet).
- Teach students to *question AI outputs* just as they would any source.

Thus, the critical challenge ahead is not merely adapting education to technological change, but fundamentally reimagining it to cultivate empowered, reflective, and ethically grounded individuals who can thrive in, and positively transform, the post-AI world. To thrive amidst this accelerating uncertainty, students must become metacognitive learners—capable of not merely mastering content but mastering the art of thinking itself. They must actively reflect upon and regulate their cognitive processes, adapting continuously to new contexts shaped by technological innovation. The future of learning is undeniably metacognitive.

To navigate and leverage the rapidly evolving AI landscape, transcend traditional compliance-based education, and achieve collective transformation, schools must intentionally embed metacognitive approaches that

- advance agency-driven approaches;
- cultivate democratically empowered, self-directed learners; and.
- position metacognitive clarity as an ethical imperative for equity.

AI + Metacognitive Prompts for Students

- *"How can I use AI to check my work without letting it do the thinking for me?"*
- *"What assumptions might this tool have built in?"*
- *"How do I know if I can trust the information AI is giving me?"*
- *"When should I ask a human for feedback instead of relying on AI?"*

Advance Agency-Driven Approaches

The World Economic Forum (WEF), in its Future of Jobs Report (2023), highlights the urgent necessity to cultivate essential competencies such as critical thinking, adaptability, complex problem-solving, self-management, resilience, leadership, collaboration, and creativity to meet the rapidly evolving demands of the post-AI workplace. The agency-driven structures detailed in Chapter 8 offer actionable frameworks categorized into learner-centered approaches and systemic approaches for instructional leadership and transformation. These structures provide concrete pathways for educators and students to thrive and lead within an AI-accelerated global context.

Learner-Centered Approaches

Learner-centered approaches prioritize direct student agency, leadership, and authentic voice, ensuring that learners are central to the transformational process:

- **Student-Led Instructional Rounds:** Students take active roles as reflective observers and analysts of instructional practices, developing critical thinking, collaboration, leadership, and self-management skills. As AI-driven technologies increase the necessity for empathetic human judgment, these student-driven assessment practices cultivate reflective leaders adept at collaborating with and enhancing AI tools.

- **Student Governance Councils:** Through explicit reflective practices embedded in democratic decision-making processes, students cultivate resilience, strategic decision-making, and adaptive governance skills. This approach fosters informed, reflective leadership capable of ethically navigating AI-driven complexities.

- **Youth Empowered Stewardship (YES):** YES leverages human-centered design and creative, reflective methodologies to develop empathy, resilience, creative resistance, and complex problem-solving skills. Students identify community needs, collaboratively design innovative AI-informed solutions, and iteratively refine their approaches—shaping adaptive, innovative thinkers who responsibly engage with AI advancements.

Moving From Compliance to Empowerment

True transformation begins when schools shift their focus from external control to learner ownership. Compliance-based systems emphasize rules, procedures, and uniform outcomes, while empowerment invites curiosity, reflection, and purposeful choice. Figure 11.1 contrasts these two mindsets, illustrating how classrooms that nurture empowerment create conditions for students to think independently, act with integrity, and take collective responsibility for their learning and community.

Figure 11.1: Compliance Versus Empowerment

Systemic Approaches for Transformation

Systemic approaches emphasize structured collaboration between adults and students, fostering transformational instructional leadership and equity-driven inquiry:

- **Collaborative Inquiry:** Utilizing structured protocols like the Evidence–Analysis–Action (EAA) framework, educators engage in reflective processes, systematically examining evidence of student learning, identifying patterns in thinking, and designing targeted instructional strategies. Instructional Leadership Teams (ILTs) play a critical role by facilitating and guiding these reflective dialogues, modeling the inquiry process, and supporting teacher teams (ideally Impact Teams) in translating insights into effective classroom practices. Impact Teams, functioning as collaborative PLCs, work interdependently with the ILT, ensuring alignment between instructional goals and school-wide priorities, creating a cohesive system of support and continuous improvement. This structured, collaborative approach, driven by the dynamic partnership between ILTs and Impact Teams, builds collective capacity for critical thinking, adaptability, and complex problem-solving, empowering educators and learners to navigate uncertainties introduced by AI flexibly.
- **Metacognitive Equity Walks:** Metacognitive equity walks focus explicitly on examining cognitive and instructional equity to address implicit biases and systemic inequities, particularly those potentially exacerbated by AI systems. Participants develop resilience, adaptive problem-solving, and ethical reasoning capacities—essential for ethically and equitably integrating AI technologies into educational contexts.

Both learner-centered and systemic approaches necessitate robust intergenerational collaboration, enabling students and adults to collaboratively shape educational environments responsive to the dynamic challenges posed by artificial intelligence. By deeply embedding metacognitive clarity within these practices, educators and learners co-create reflective, adaptive, collaborative, and ethically minded competencies essential for meaningful democratic engagement and sustained success in our complex, AI-driven world.

Reflect deeply:

- How effectively are our current instructional practices embedding opportunities for students to explicitly practice and reflect upon critical thinking, adaptability, and ethical reasoning as shaped by the rise of AI?
- In what ways do our schools' leadership and governance structures genuinely empower students to collaboratively evaluate, adapt, and ethically navigate challenges posed by AI rather than merely providing token participation?
- What specific evidence indicates that the metacognitive approaches described (Collaborative Inquiry, Student-Led Instructional Rounds, Metacognitive Equity Walks, Student Governance Councils, and YES) are directly supporting learners in developing agency-driven competencies essential to thriving in AI-influenced contexts?

Cultivate Democratically Empowered, Self-Directed Learners

We can cultivate democratically empowered, self-directed learners by explicitly teaching students to engage deeply in reflective decision-making, collaboration, and leadership. These essential competencies equip learners with the critical literacy and reflective capacities required to leverage AI responsibly and effectively.

Democratically empowered learners actively co-design their educational journeys, driven by reflective goal setting, student-led assessments, inclusive decision-making processes, and impactful frameworks such as those mentioned in Chapter 8. AI tools enhance these practices by offering personalized feedback, data-driven insights, and opportunities for learners to self-assess and adjust their pathways in real time, thereby promoting deeper metacognitive engagement.

When we effectively integrate AI within these democratic structures, we create vibrant, adaptive spaces within schools where students authentically practice civic skills and technological literacy, building essential capacities such as critical reflection, adaptive problem-solving, collaborative decision-making, and ethical AI use. Regular engagement in reflective processes, augmented by AI-driven analytics and support systems, develops learners' metacognitive clarity, preparing them to navigate increasingly complex challenges, construct meaningful learning pathways, and assume active roles as morally and ethically centered creators—not passive consumers—of knowledge and technology.

The transformative potential of democratically empowered, AI-literate learners extends far beyond classrooms, positively influencing communities and societies. When students genuinely participate in shaping their educational experiences and critically engage with AI technologies, they build a profound sense of agency, digital citizenship, and responsibility. This directly translates into informed, empathetic, and proactive community engagement. Such an empowered approach not only prepares learners to thrive individually but also equips them to contribute meaningfully to collective transformation, fostering societal resilience and sustained democratic growth in an AI-rich future.

Reflect deeply:

- Which democratic strategies highlighted throughout this book could most immediately enhance learner empowerment and responsible AI engagement in your educational context?

- In what ways could fostering self-directed, AI-literate learners strengthen community engagement, societal contributions, and democratic resilience?

Tools for a Metacognitive Future

Want to put these ideas into practice? See the Online Appendices for reproducible tools and templates, including:

- **AI + Metacognitive Reflection Cards** – prompts to help students use AI as a thinking partner, not a replacement.
- **Civic Reflection Cards** – routines for detecting misinformation and building digital discernment.
- **Ethical Guardrails for AI** – a checklist for leaders and teachers to ensure equity in AI use.
- **Future Competencies Table** – links WEF 2035 skills to metacognitive practices.
- **Student-Led Civic Hackathon Protocol** – a step-by-step guide for running democratic, problem-solving events with students in the lead.
- All tools can be found in the online appendices.

Position Metacognitive Clarity as an Ethical Imperative for Equity

Metacognitive clarity also carries an ethical dimension; in fact, we would go so far as to call it a moral imperative. Throughout this book, we've emphasized the essential function of reflection in metacognitive clarity, and this includes reflecting on our responsibilities as educators to ensure all students have equitable opportunities to thrive. Ethics involves discerning right from wrong and choosing actions that enhance fairness, dignity, and respect for all individuals. The World Economic Forum emphasizes that equitable access to quality education significantly influences positive global economic and social outcomes (2023, p. 31)—all the more reason to position metacognitive clarity as an ethical obligation.

Saundra McGuire's concept of "metacognitive equity" underscores this ethical imperative, describing the urgent need to close the gap between students equipped with effective metacognitive strategies and those who don't have access to them (McGuire, 2021). She argues convincingly that disparities in academic performance often reflect differences in students' exposure to and mastery of metacognitive skills, not inherent ability or potential. Metacognitive inequities perpetuate systemic injustice and limit the potential of marginalized students. The key to disrupting these inequities is to empower our students with metacognitive strategies, such as reflection, self-questioning, and strategic adjustment. In this way, they gain agency over their learning, fostering a deeper sense of belonging and capability (McGuire, 2021).

Reflect deeply:

- How could metacognitive clarity help uncover and address hidden inequities in your educational setting?
- What immediate actions can you take today to ensure all students experience genuine belonging and equitable opportunities for metacognitive development?

Clarity Against Misinformation: A Civic and Metacognitive Skill

As mentioned in Chapters 1 and 6, we live in a world where the truth is increasingly contested; in this post-truth era, teaching students to detect misinformation is a civic responsibility. Misinformation spreads faster than facts, fueled by emotion, algorithms, and the deliberate erosion of trust in democratic institutions. In 2018, MIT researchers found that false stories spread six times faster on social media than true ones—particularly when they provoke strong emotional reactions like anger or fear (Vosoughi, Roy, & Aral, 2018). And the stakes couldn't be higher: Consider that in 2023, Fox News paid $787 million to settle a defamation lawsuit for knowingly spreading election-related misinformation. This is the landscape our students now live—and learn—in. And metacognitive clarity may be one of the most powerful tools we can give them.

Metacognitive Literacy Is Misinformation Resistance

Detecting misinformation isn't just a technical skill—it's a reflective discipline. It requires learners to slow down, question their impulses, and intentionally examine how they process information. By engaging in the metacognitive cycle—planning, monitoring, and evaluating their thinking—students develop the habits of mind needed to resist manipulation, assess credibility, and respond thoughtfully.

Reflection Builds Resistance to Misinformation

When students pause to question, verify, and reflect before reacting, they activate executive brain systems that support critical thinking and emotional regulation. These routines strengthen cognitive flexibility and help learners resist manipulation (Diamond, 2013; Zelazo & Lyons, 2012). The following questions exemplify how this cycle equips students to think critically and act ethically in an age saturated with digital noise.

- **Plan:** "Why am I reading this? What's my purpose, and what do I already know?"
- **Monitor:** "How does this make me feel? Am I reacting emotionally? Could that be intentional?"
- **Evaluate:** "Who created this content, and for what purpose? Can I verify it through another source?"

These are not merely cognitive strategies. They are deeply *metacognitive acts*—acts of resistance, discernment, and self-regulation in an era designed to distract and divide.

Digital Civics and Global Leadership

Some nations have already recognized this urgency. Finland, for example, has integrated media literacy and misinformation detection into its national curriculum. Students are explicitly taught to evaluate bias, verify claims, and detect propaganda as early as primary school (OECD, 2021). In the United States, ISTE's Digital Citizenship Standards call on students to "evaluate the accuracy, perspective, credibility, and relevance of information" they encounter (ISTE, 2016). These frameworks are not simply about responsible technology use—they are about empowering students to be reflective, ethical participants in democracy.

Metacognitive Equity and the Threat of Misinformation

Misinformation does not affect all learners equally. Communities already marginalized by systemic inequities often bear the most significant burden—from misleading health information targeting multilingual families to algorithmic bias that silences dissent. When students aren't taught how to think about their thinking—how to question, source-check, and emotionally regulate—they are left unprotected against these forces.

This is why metacognitive clarity is an equity issue. It closes the gap between students who consume information passively and those who interrogate it actively. It bridges the divide between those vulnerable to manipulation and those empowered to think independently.

Students need more than fact-checking skills to resist misinformation, they need metacognitive clarity to pause, reflect, and examine their own thinking. For practical insights and classroom strategies, read our blog posts, "Metacognitive Clarity: The Secret Weapon Against Misinformation" and "Stop the Spin—Use AI to Fact-Check Memes" in our *Further Reading* section of the General Resources appendices.

Civic Reflection in Action: Student Prompts

To build resistance to misinformation, students need more than content knowledge—they need metacognitive habits that help them question, reflect, and discern. Civic reflection equips learners to pause, examine their emotional responses, and evaluate information with clarity and care. The prompts below support these habits, helping students become more thoughtful, ethical, and engaged participants in a rapidly evolving information landscape. To foster metacognitive resistance to misinformation, consider these prompts:

- What makes this source trustworthy—or not?
- How is this information making me feel—and why?
- What evidence is this claim based on? Can I verify it?
- What perspectives are missing? Whose voices are left out?
- Have I cross-checked this information with another reliable source?

These questions don't just build better learners—they build civic resilience. If the future of learning is truly metacognitive, then the future of democracy depends on it.

Let's teach students not only how to learn—but how to discern.

Misinformation is a storm, and metacognitive clarity is the lighthouse. Leadership guides learners safely toward a future defined by agency, equity, and collective possibility. There are more learning experiences anchored in detecting misinformation in the appendices.

Civic Reflection Prompts for Detecting Misinformation

- *What makes this source trustworthy—or not?*
- *How is this information making me feel—and why?*
- *Whose voices are included? Whose are missing?*
- *Can I verify this through another reliable source?*

Be Part of the Metacognitive Transformation

Simon Sinek famously reminds us that people don't buy what we do; they buy why we do it (2009). In education, our "why" is profoundly clear: to nurture empowered, reflective individuals capable of thriving in a complex, rapidly changing world. Throughout this book, you've explored powerful approaches to metacognitive clarity, each essential for genuine educational transformation.

This book is an invitation to educators, leaders, and advocates to actively participate in this critical shift toward a metacognitive future. Embracing metacognitive clarity as an ethical imperative positions you to address systemic inequities, amplify student voice, and cultivate authentic democratic engagement. Your intentional actions today profoundly shape tomorrow's learners, leaders, and citizens.

Hope and Imagination Drive Learning Forward

When students envision themselves making a difference in the future, brain systems responsible for imagination and ethical reasoning, like the default mode network, activate. This helps learners connect today's actions to tomorrow's possibilities (Immordino-Yang, 2016; Tamir et al., 2017).

Imagine the future of education as akin to constructing a bridge. Each learner equipped with metacognitive clarity contributes a vital beam and reinforces the structure through reflective insights, critical questioning, and self-regulation. Together, these beams form a resilient pathway, enabling all students to confidently cross from today'›s uncertainties toward a future defined by agency, equity, and limitless potential.

A 30–60–90-Day Plan for Scaling Metacognitive Clarity

Metacognitive clarity becomes real when it moves from theory into everyday practice. Scaling it across a classroom, grade level, or whole school requires a *gradual release*: start with shared language, move into guided practice, and end with student ownership. This simple 30–60–90-Day Plan provides a roadmap for how students, teachers, leaders, and families can work in sync to make thinking visible and coachable.

Phase 1 (0–30 Days): Shared Language of Learning

- *Students:* Use everyday examples (sports, arts, home life) to name goals and strategies.
- *Teachers:* Model metacognition through think-alouds beyond academics.
- *Leaders:* Frame the "why" and supply common visuals/tools.
- *Families:* Try one reflection prompt at home ("What's your plan before starting?").

Phase 2 (31–60 Days): Guided Practice in Academics

- *Students:* Engage in think-alouds, label strategies, and track progress with checklists.
- *Teachers:* Embed Plan–Monitor–Adjust pauses and co-construct success criteria.
- *Leaders:* Focus walk-throughs on student use of metacognitive language.
- *Families:* Learn simple academic think-alouds to use during homework.

Phase 3 (61–90 Days): Student Ownership of the Cycle

- *Students:* Frame learning goals, self-assess, and share evidence of progress.
- *Teachers:* Shift from modeling to facilitating; highlight strategy use in feedback.
- *Leaders:* Showcase student voice and adjust systems to allow time for reflection.
- *Families:* Participate in student-led conferences where learners explain their growth through the metacognitive cycle.

By the end of 90 days, the routines of naming goals, selecting strategies, checking effectiveness, and adjusting course become shared habits. These habits drive both rigor (students choosing and adapting strategies) and democracy (students using evidence and voice to guide their learning).

Reflect and Act

This week, reflect: How prepared are your students—not just to learn content, but to *discern* truth, act ethically, and adapt in an AI-driven world?

Choose one action to move from theory to transformation:

- **Integrate misinformation detection** → Embed prompts like *"What makes this source trustworthy?"* or *"How is this making me feel—and why?"* into everyday learning routines. Remember: *Misinformation is a storm, and metacognitive clarity is the lighthouse.*

- **Deepen student voice in practice** → Launch or refine student-led instructional rounds or governance councils that position learners as co-analysts of teaching, technology, and equity.

- **Strengthen collaborative inquiry** → Use the Evidence–Analysis–Action cycle in PLCs or Impact Teams to examine not just outcomes but *how students are thinking*.

- **Conduct equity checks** → Run metacognitive equity walks to surface who is—and isn't—being positioned as a reflective thinker in AI-supported classrooms.

- **Embed reflective goal setting** → Regularly invite students to plan, monitor, and evaluate their growth as both learners and citizens.

The future of learning—and democracy itself—depends on it. So let's teach students not only how to learn, but how to discern.

FROM DREAM TO POSSIBILITY

When we wrote this book, we were dreaming of what the possibilities would be if schools pointed their compass to metacognitive clarity. We are dreaming of what schools could be if metacognition were not an add-on, but the throughline of learning.

- **Personal Level:** The dream begins with the individual. After all, each of us can only truly control ourselves. When I use the cycle—Plan → Monitor → Evaluate → Adjust—I take ownership of my growth. Research shows that this kind of self-regulation has one of the most substantial impacts on learning (Hattie, 2010). At its core, reflection is about more than results—it shapes confidence, identity, and direction.
- **Classroom Level:** Students no longer guess their way through tasks—they plan intentionally, monitor progress, and adjust with evidence. Teachers act as coaches, modeling strategies and naming the "why" behind them. Formative assessment becomes fuel for agency (Wiliam, 2011).
- **School Level:** Implementation science warns that initiative fatigue erodes trust and sustainability (Fullan, 2016). By infusing metacognition into what schools already do well, initiatives connect rather than compete. PLCs and ILTs focus on evidence of student thinking, not just scores.
- **System Level:** Schools become adaptive learning organizations (Senge, 1990). Leaders model reflection and adjustment, creating structures where feedback loops guide improvement. MTSS (Multi-Tiered System of Supports), UDL, SEL, and PBL (Problem and Project-Based Learning) are no longer silos—they are connected through the metacognitive cycle (Fixsen et al., 2005).
- **Societal Level:** A generation raised in metacognition grows into citizens who question assumptions, weigh evidence, reflect on bias, and adjust their actions. They carry the habits of self-regulation, criticality, and collective agency (CASEL, 2020; Ladson-Billings, 1995). Assets are emphasized and relationships are central. In this way, metacognition strengthens not only learning but democracy itself.

This is our dream: beginning personally with each learner's inner voice, radiating outward into classrooms, schools, systems, and society. It is a dream of coherence, agency, and clarity—built step by step, reflection by reflection, adjustment by adjustment.

AN INVITATION TO METACOGNITIVE TRANSFORMATION

Beyond the insights and strategies we've shared throughout this book, our greatest aspiration is that educators and leaders feel empowered to bring the transformative power of metacognitive clarity to life in every learning community. It's now time for us to translate our collective wisdom into deliberate, meaningful action by amplifying your voice, the voices of our learners, and the communities we serve. As educators, we possess the remarkable ability and profound responsibility to nurture learners who are self-aware, empowered, and equipped to thoughtfully navigate and shape the world around them.

To become agents of metacognitive transformation, we must commit ourselves deeply and authentically to this reflective practice. We hope that this book ignites your desire to foster spaces where learners confidently engage in the metacognitive cycle: planning, monitoring, and evaluating their thinking and actions. But desire alone is insufficient—only through intentional, collective action can we achieve the enduring transformation our students deserve.

Here are 10 invitations for creating a movement anchored in metacognitive clarity; our students deserve this, and our future demands it.

1. **Have the Courage to Reflect:** Even as experienced educators, each of us is on a continuous journey of growth. Embrace vulnerability in examining your instructional practices, biases, and assumptions, and invite learners, families, and caregivers to do the same. Our collective growth emerges from a culture of courageous reflection where every voice is valued.

2. **Amplify Learner Voice:** Regularly invite students to articulate their thinking, question assumptions, and co-construct learning goals. Deep clarity emerges when we also listen deeply to families and caregivers, honoring their lived experiences as foundational to learning and weaving their insights into classroom practice.

3. **Commit to Empathy:** Foster authentic connections by intentionally modeling empathy. Understanding the emotional landscapes of our learners—and the families and caregivers who support them—builds trust, deepens relationships, and strengthens the reflective communities essential for meaningful learning.

4. **Embrace Identity and Belonging:** Every learner brings a unique mosaic of identities to our classrooms. Elevate practices that affirm diverse cultural, linguistic, and personal

strengths, and extend this affirmation to families and caregivers. When both students and their families feel seen, heard, and valued, inclusive environments flourish.

5. **Share Leadership:** Metacognitive clarity thrives in democratic spaces. Actively engage students, families, and caregivers in decision-making, goal setting, and co-assessment processes. Shared leadership builds agency across the entire learning community and reinforces the belief that we are partners in student success.

6. **Lead With Integrity:** Inspire others by embodying metacognitive clarity in your professional practice. Conscious, reflective leadership fosters environments where innovation, transparency, and continuous improvement flourish—and signals to students and families that integrity is at the core of school culture.

7. **Educate Collaboratively:** Form inquiry groups, book studies, or reflective circles focused on advancing metacognitive clarity. Invite families and caregivers to participate in authentic ways. Collective inquiry multiplies our impact, strengthens partnerships, and creates sustainable change that is community-wide.

8. **Be Bold in Action:** Identify one metacognitive practice to enhance or innovate intentionally. Take measured risks and embrace imperfections; each attempt moves us closer to clarity and deeper understanding. Share both successes and challenges with families and caregivers so they can learn with us and alongside their children.

9. **Spread Awareness:** Utilize social media, blogs, videos, or community forums to share your metacognitive journey. Spotlight the voices of students and families, and connect with networks committed to reflective practices. Amplify your impact by learning and growing together publicly.

10. **Reflect Together:** Regularly revisit and refine your approach to metacognitive clarity through collaborative reflection. Include families and caregivers in this cycle of reflection to ensure continuous growth, responsiveness, and alignment with the evolving needs of students, classrooms, and communities.

We are stronger together because we truly belong to each other.

Paul J. Bloomberg, Isaac Wells, and St. Claire Adriaan

GLOSSARY

agency: Learners' capacity and willingness to take purposeful initiative, ownership, and accountability for their learning through goal setting, reflection, and strategic decision-making.

assessment for learning (AfL): Ongoing assessment practices that make learning visible and guide instruction, with students serving as active partners in self-assessment, feedback, and reflection.

asset-based pedagogy: An educational approach that recognizes, affirms, and leverages learners' cultural, linguistic, and experiential strengths as assets for learning.

belonging: The experience of being appreciated, validated, accepted, and treated fairly within a learning community, serving as a foundational condition for engagement, risk-taking, and rigorous thinking.

clarity of ownership: The cultivation of learner agency through goal setting, reflection, co-assessment, and shared responsibility for learning.

clarity of process: Explicit instruction in learning-to-learn strategies that help learners plan, monitor, and evaluate their thinking across tasks, disciplines, and contexts.

clarity of purpose: Alignment of learning goals with personal meaning, academic expectations, and community relevance to support justice-centered, democratic learning.

co-assessment: A collaborative assessment process in which students and teachers jointly evaluate learning evidence to strengthen metacognition, ownership, and mutual accountability.

co-construction: The shared creation of learning intentions, success criteria, and assessment processes by educators and learners.

collaborative inquiry: A shared process in which educators and learners analyze evidence of learning to surface thinking patterns and determine responsive instructional actions.

collective efficacy: A shared belief that a group's collaborative efforts can positively influence learning outcomes.

criticality: The ability to examine context, power, and systems in order to question assumptions, evaluate perspectives, and engage in equity-focused analysis.

culturally responsive teaching (CRT): Instructional practices that affirm learners' cultural identities and integrate lived experiences as assets for engagement and understanding.

democratic learning environment: A learning space characterized by shared power, student voice, collective responsibility, and participation in meaningful decision-making.

Dual Capacity-Building Framework: A framework for strengthening family–school partnerships by building the skills, knowledge, confidence, and relational trust of both educators and families to support student learning and agency.

equity walks: Reflective walkthroughs focused on identifying patterns of access, participation, and opportunity to inform more equitable practices.

evaluate: The metacognitive stage in which learners reflect on outcomes, assess strategy effectiveness, and determine next steps for improvement.

Evidence–Analysis–Action (EAA) Framework: A structured process used by Impact Teams to analyze evidence of learning and translate insights into instructional action.

identity affirmation: Intentional practices that recognize and value learners' cultural, linguistic, and personal identities as central to engagement, agency, and metacognitive growth.

Impact Teams: Collaborative professional learning teams that use inquiry, evidence, and reflection to strengthen instruction and learner agency.

learning intentions: Clear, learner-friendly statements that describe the purpose, relevance, and intended outcomes of learning.

learning-to-learn strategies: Strategies that help learners manage cognition, effort, and reflection, enabling transfer across subjects and situations.

metacognition: Awareness and regulation of one's thinking through intentional planning, monitoring, and evaluating of learning.

metacognitive clarity: A justice-centered practice that empowers learners to understand how and why they learn, enabling agency, reflection, and democratic participation.

metacognitive cycle: An iterative process of planning, monitoring, and evaluating that guides learning, reflection, and decision-making.

metacognitive equity: Ensuring all learners have access to metacognitive tools and strategies that support agency, voice, and self-directed learning.

metacognitive equity walks: Observational practices that examine how metacognitive opportunities are distributed and experienced across learners.

micro-teaching: A professional learning approach in which educators practice specific instructional strategies in focused settings and receive targeted feedback.

monitor: The metacognitive stage in which learners track progress, adjust strategies, and manage attention and effort during learning.

peer assessment: A process in which learners use shared success criteria to evaluate and provide feedback on one another's work.

peer coaching: A collaborative professional learning approach in which educators observe, reflect, and refine practice together.

plan: The metacognitive stage in which learners set goals, activate prior knowledge, anticipate challenges, and select strategies.

professional learning community (PLC): A collaborative group of educators who engage in ongoing inquiry around evidence of student learning to improve practice.

psychological safety: The shared belief that individuals can take risks, reflect openly, and share thinking without fear of judgment or ridicule.

rigor: Meaningful cognitive challenge that promotes deep thinking, transfer, and learner ownership rather than compliance or task completion.

student governance councils: Student-led structures that support shared leadership, voice, and democratic participation in school communities.

student-led instructional rounds: Structured opportunities for students to observe instruction, reflect on learning practices, and contribute to improvement efforts.

success criteria: Clear, co-constructed descriptions of what quality learning looks like, used to guide self-assessment and feedback.

Universal Design for Learning (UDL): A framework for designing flexible, inclusive learning experiences that reduce barriers and honor learner variability.

Youth Empowered Stewardship (YES): An intergenerational partnership model that positions youth as leaders and advocates who use reflection, agency, and collaboration to advance equity and community well-being.

REFERENCES

Alencastre, M., & Kawaiʻaeʻa, K. (2018). ʻŌiwi leadership: Indigenous teacher education in Hawaiʻi. In S. E. Evans et al. (Eds.), *Indigenous leadership in education*.

Ambrose, S. A., Bridges, M. W., DiPietro, M., Lovett, M. C., & Norman, M. K. (2010). *How learning works: Seven research-based principles for smart teaching*. Jossey-Bass.

Baldwin, J. (1965). *The White Man's Guilt*. In J. Baldwin, Collected Essays (T. Morrison, Ed., pp. 722–731). Library of America.

Bandura, A. (1997). *Self-efficacy: The exercise of control*. W. H. Freeman.

Barnhardt, R., & Kawagley, A. O. (2005). Indigenous knowledge systems and Alaska Native ways of knowing. *Anthropology & Education Quarterly, 36*(1), 8–23.

Baumeister, R. F., & Vohs, K. D. (2011). Self-regulation and the executive function: The self as controlling agent. In K. D. Vohs & R. F. Baumeister (Eds.), *Handbook of self-regulation: Research, theory, and applications* (2nd ed., pp. 180–197). Guilford Press.

Benjamin, R. (2019). *Race after technology: Abolitionist tools for the new Jim code*. Polity Press.

Berliner, D. C. (1986). In pursuit of the expert pedagogue. *Educational Researcher, 15*(7), 5–13.

Best, J. R., Miller, P. H., & Jones, L. L. (2011). Executive functions after age 5: Changes and correlates. *Developmental Review, 31*(4), 221–238. https://doi.org/10.1016/j.dr.2011.09.002

Black, P., & Wiliam, D. (2009). Developing the theory of formative assessment. *Educational Assessment, Evaluation and Accountability, 21*, 5–31.

Blair, C., & Diamond, A. (2008). Biological processes in prevention and intervention: The promotion of self-regulation as a means of preventing school failure. *Development and Psychopathology, 20*(3), 899–911. https://doi.org/10.1017/S0954579408000436

Bloomberg, P. J., & Pitchford, B. (2016). *Leading impact teams: Building a culture of efficacy*. Corwin Press.

Bloomberg, P. J., & Pitchford, B. (2023). *Leading impact teams: Building a culture of efficacy and agency*. Corwin Press.

Bloomberg, P. J., Vandas, K., Twyman, I., Dukes, V., Carrillo Fairchild, R., Hamilton, C., & Wells, I. (2022). *Amplify learner voice through culturally responsive and sustaining assessment*. Mimi & Todd Press.

Boldt, A., & Gilbert, S. J. (2022). Metacognition and the social brain. *Cognition, 224*, 105071.

Brown, A. L. (1977). Metacognitive development and reading. In R. J. Spiro, B. C. Bruce, & W. F. Brewer (Eds.), *Theoretical issues in reading comprehension* (pp. 453–481). Erlbaum.

Brown, A. L., Bransford, J. D., Ferrara, R. A., & Campione, J. C. (1981). Learning, remembering, and understanding. In J. H. Flavell & E. M. Markman (Eds.), *Handbook of child psychology* (Vol. 3, pp. 77–166). Wiley.

Bruner, J. S. (1966). *Toward a theory of instruction*. Harvard University Press.

Brynjolfsson, E., & McAfee, A. (2017). *Machine, platform, crowd: Harnessing our digital future*. W. W. Norton & Company.

Cajete, G. (1994). *Look to the mountain: An ecology of Indigenous education*. Kivaki Press.

Center for Educational Leadership. (n.d.). *The 5D+ instructional framework*. University of Washington. https://k12leadership.washington.edu/

Collaborative for Academic, Social, and Emotional Learning. (n.d.). *CASEL framework*. https://casel.org/frameworks/

Collaborative for Academic, Social, and Emotional Learning. (2020). *What is SEL?* https://casel.org/fundamentals-of-sel/

Costa, A. L., & Kallick, B. (2008). *Learning and leading with habits of mind: 16 essential characteristics for success*. ASCD.

Darling-Hammond, L. (2019). *Learning to teach for deeper learning: Competency-based teacher education*. Harvard Education Press.

Dee, T. S., & Penner, E. K. (2017). The causal effects of cultural relevance: Evidence from an ethnic studies curriculum. *American Educational Research Journal, 54*(1), 127–166. https://doi.org/10.3102/0002831216677002

Dewey, J. (1910). *How we think*. D. C. Heath.

Diamond, A. (2013). Executive functions. *Annual Review of Psychology, 64*, 135–168. https://doi.org/10.1146/annurev-psych-113011-143750

Donohoo, J. (2013). *Collaborative inquiry for educators: A facilitator's guide to school improvement*. Corwin Press.

Duckworth, A. L., & Carlson, S. M. (2012). Self-regulation and school success. In B. W. Sokol, F. M. E. Grouzet, & U. Müller (Eds.), *Self-regulation and autonomy* (pp. 208–230). Cambridge University Press.

Durlak, J. A., Weissberg, R. P., Dymnicki, A. B., Taylor, R. D., & Schellinger, K. B. (2011). The impact of enhancing students' social and emotional learning: A meta-analysis. *Child Development, 82*(1), 405–432. https://doi.org/10.1111/j.1467-8624.2010.01564.x

Dweck, C. S. (2008). *Mindset: The new psychology of success*. Random House.

Efklides, A. (2011). Interactions of metacognition with motivation and affect in self-regulated learning: The MASRL model. *Educational Psychologist, 46*(1), 6–25.

Efklides, A. (2012). The role of metacognitive experiences in the learning process. In A. Efklides & P. Misailidi (Eds.), *Trends and prospects in metacognition research*. Springer.

Eubanks, V. (2018). *Automating inequality: How high-tech tools profile, police, and punish the poor*. St. Martin's Press.

Falchikov, N. (2005). *Improving assessment through student involvement*. RoutledgeFalmer.

Fixsen, D. L., Naoom, S. F., Blase, K. A., Friedman, R. M., & Wallace, F. (2005). *Implementation research: A synthesis of the literature*. National Implementation Research Network.

Flavell, J. H. (1976). *Metacognitive aspects of problem solving*. In L. B. Resnick (Ed.), *The nature of intelligence* (pp. 231–235). Lawrence Erlbaum Associates.

Flavell, J. H., Miller, P. H., & Miller, S. A. (1985). *Cognitive development*. Prentice Hall.

Fleming, S. M., & Dolan, R. J. (2012). The neural basis of metacognitive ability. *Philosophical Transactions of the Royal Society B: Biological Sciences, 367*(1594), 1338–1349.

Freire, P. (1970). *Pedagogy of the oppressed*. Continuum.

Frith, C. D. (2012). The role of metacognition in human social interactions. *Philosophical Transactions of the Royal Society B, 367*, 2213–2223.

Fullan, M. (2016). *The new meaning of educational change* (5th ed.). Teachers College Press.

García, O., & Kleifgen, J. A. (2018). *Educating emergent bilinguals* (2nd ed.). Teachers College Press.

Gholson, M. L., & Martin, D. B. (2019). Mathematics as a civil right: Equity as liberation. *Journal for Research in Mathematics Education, 50*(4), 330–336.

Gottlieb, M. (2016). *Assessing English language learners: Bridges to educational equity*. Corwin Press.

Hammond, Z. (2015). *Culturally responsive teaching and the brain*. Corwin Press.

Hargreaves, A., & Fullan, M. (2012). *Professional capital: Transforming teaching in every school*. Teachers College Press.

Hattie, J. (2010). *Visible learning*. Routledge.

Hattie, J. (2012). *Visible learning for teachers*. Routledge.

Hattie, J., & Donoghue, G. (2016). Learning strategies: A synthesis and conceptual model. *NPJ Science of Learning, 1*, 16013.

Henderson, A. T., & Mapp, K. L. (2002). *A new wave of evidence: The impact of school, family, and community connections on student achievement*. Southwest Educational Development Laboratory.

hooks, b. (1994). *Teaching to transgress*. Routledge.

Immordino-Yang, M. H. (2016). *Emotions, learning, and the brain*. W. W. Norton & Company.

Immordino-Yang, M. H., & Damasio, A. (2007). We feel, therefore we learn. *Mind, Brain, and Education, 1*(1), 3–10.

International Society for Technology in Education. (2016). *ISTE standards for students*. ISTE.

Irimoto, T. (2004). Inuit-Qallunaat pedagogies and the development of cultural competence. *Arctic Anthropology, 41*(2), 1–15.

Jagers, R. J., Rivas-Drake, D., & Williams, B. (2019). Transformative social and emotional learning. *Educational Psychologist, 54*(3), 162–184.

Jensen, B., Sonnemann, J., Roberts-Hull, K., & Hunter, A. (2016). *Beyond PD: Teacher professional learning in high-performing systems*. National Center on Education and the Economy.

Killion, J. (2023). *Assessing impact: Evaluating staff development* (3rd ed.). Corwin Press.

Koenecke, A., et al. (2020). Racial disparities in automated speech recognition. *Proceedings of the National Academy of Sciences, 117*(14), 7684–7689.

Ladson-Billings, G. (1995). Toward a theory of culturally relevant pedagogy. *American Educational Research Journal, 32*(3), 465–491.

Lawrence-Lightfoot, S. (2003). *The essential conversation*. Random House.

Learning for Justice. (2016). *Social justice standards: The teaching tolerance anti-bias framework*. Learning for Justice.

Learning Forward. (2022). *Standards for professional learning*. Learning Forward.

Leithwood, K. (1992). The principal's role in teacher development. In M. Fullan & A. Hargreaves (Eds.), *Teacher development and educational change* (pp. 86–103). Falmer Press.

Lieberman, M. D. (2013). *Social: Why our brains are wired to connect*. Crown.

Mapp, K. L., & Bergman, E. (2019). *Dual capacity-building framework for family–school partnerships* (Version 2). U.S. Department of Education.

Marcus, E., et al. (2020). Self-relevance enhances memory for information. *Journal of Experimental Psychology: General, 149*(9), 1709–1725.

McClelland, M. M., & Cameron, C. E. (2012). Self-regulation in early childhood. *Child Development Perspectives, 6*(2), 136–142.

McDowell, M., & Eisberg, A. (2024). *A visual, step-by-step guide for re-envisioning rigor: Powerful routines for promoting student agency*. Mimi & Todd Press.

McGuire, S. Y., & McGuire, S. (2015). *Teach students how to learn: Strategies you can incorporate into any course to improve student metacognition, study skills, and motivation*. Stylus Publishing.

Meltzer, L. (2010). *Promoting executive function in the classroom: What works for special-needs learners*. Guilford Press.

Moll, L. C., Amanti, C., Neff, D., & González, N. (1992). Funds of knowledge. *Theory Into Practice, 31*(2), 132–141.

Muhammad, G. (2020). *Cultivating genius: An equity framework for culturally and historically responsive literacy.*. Scholastic.

Murayama, K., Pekrun, R., Lichtenfeld, S., & vom Hofe, R. (2010). Predicting long-term growth in students' mathematics achievement: The role of motivation. *Journal of Educational Psychology, 102*(3), 597–610.

Nasir, N. S., & Hand, V. (2008). From the court to the classroom. *Review of Educational Research, 78*(2), 264–309.

National Foundation for Educational Research. (2023). *The skills imperative 2035*. NFER.

Nelson, T. O., & Narens, L. (1990). Metamemory. In G. H. Bower (Ed.), *The psychology of learning and motivation* (Vol. 26, pp. 125–173). Academic Press.

Noble, S. U. (2018). *Algorithms of oppression: How search engines reinforce racism*. New York University Press.

O'Neil, C. (2016). *Weapons of math destruction: How big data increases inequality and threatens democracy*. Crown.

Organisation for Economic Co-operation and Development. (2021). *Future of education and skills 2030*. OECD Publishing.

Oyserman, D., & Destin, M. (2010). Identity-based motivation. *Perspectives on Psychological Science, 5*(6), 702–717.

Ozer, E. J. (2017). Youth-led participatory action research: Developmental and equity perspectives. *Advances in Child Development and Behavior, 52*, 189–207.

Paris, D., & Alim, H. S. (2017). *Culturally sustaining pedagogies*. Teachers College Press.

Paris, S. G., & Winograd, P. (1992). How metacognition can promote academic learning and instruction. In B. Jones & L. Idol (Eds.), *Dimensions of thinking and cognitive instruction* (pp. 15–51). Erlbaum.

Pintrich, P. R. (2002). The role of metacognitive knowledge in learning, teaching, and assessing. *Theory Into Practice, 41*(4), 219–225.

Powell, W. (2019). *Courageous leadership: Shaping schools by focusing on purpose and people*. Solution Tree Press.

Psencik, K., Brown, F., & Hirsh, S. (2020). *Becoming a learning system*. Learning Forward.

Quigley, A., Muijs, D., & Stringer, E. (2018). *Metacognition and self-regulated learning: Guidance report*. Education Endowment Foundation.

Ritchhart, R., Church, M., & Morrison, K. (2011). *Making thinking visible*. Jossey-Bass.

Rosenshine, B., & Stevens, R. (1986). Teaching functions. In M. C. Wittrock (Ed.), *Handbook of research on teaching* (3rd ed., pp. 376–391). Macmillan.

Schraw, G., & Dennison, R. S. (1994). Assessing metacognitive awareness. *Contemporary Educational Psychology*, *19*, 460–475.

Selwyn, N. (2021). *Should robots replace teachers? AI and the future of education*. Polity Press.

Senge, P. M. (1990). *The fifth discipline*. Doubleday.

Sinek, S. (2009). *Start with why: How great leaders inspire everyone to take action*. Portfolio.

Sweller, J., Ayres, P., & Kalyuga, S. (2011). *Cognitive load theory*. Springer.

Tamir, D. I., Zaki, J., & Mitchell, J. P. (2017). Self-disclosure and the intrinsic value of sharing information. *Proceedings of the National Academy of Sciences*, *114*(6), 1465–1470.

Tatum, B. D. (2000). *Why are all the Black kids sitting together in the cafeteria?* Basic Books.

Topping, K. (1998). Peer assessment between students in schools and colleges. *Review of Educational Research*, *68*(3), 249–276.

Veas, A., Castejón, J. L., Miñano, P., & Gilar-Corbí, R. (2019). Metacognition and academic achievement. *Educational Psychology*, *39*(1), 17–37.

Vosoughi, S., Roy, D., & Aral, S. (2018). The spread of true and false news online. *Science*, *359*(6380), 1146–1151.

Warschauer, M., & Matuchniak, T. (2010). New technology and digital worlds: Analyzing evidence of equity in access, use, and outcomes. *Review of Research in Education*, *34*(1), 179–225.

Wiliam, D. (2011). *Embedded formative assessment*. Solution Tree Press.

Wiredu, K. (2004). *Cultural universals and particulars: An African perspective*. Indiana University Press.

World Economic Forum. (2023). *The future of jobs report 2023*. World Economic Forum.

Wormeli, R. (2018). *Fair isn't always equal: Assessing and grading in the differentiated classroom* (2nd ed.). Stenhouse.

Yeager, D. S., & Dweck, C. S. (2012). Mindsets that promote resilience: When students believe that personal characteristics can be developed. *Educational Psychologist*, *47*(4), 302–314.

Yunkaporta, T. (2019). *Sand talk*. HarperCollins.

Zelazo, P. D., & Carlson, S. M. (2012). Hot and cool executive function. *Child Development Perspectives*, *6*(4), 354–360.

Zimmerman, B. J. (2002). Becoming a self-regulated learner. *Theory Into Practice*, *41*(2), 64–70.

INDEX

Academia Avance Charter School case study, 146–147

academic mindset, defined, 30

academic performance, 61, 146, 156

advisory councils, 145, 146, 147

agency and autonomy
    defined, 17, 30
    family-school partnerships, 148
    future of learning and, 151–152
    Learner Agency Tree, 27–29
    professional learning for democratic agency, 130–132

AI + Metacognitive Reflection Cards, 156

AI technology, 149–152. *See also* future of learning

Alternate Perspectives strategy, 97

Amplify Learner Voice (Bloomberg et al.), 18

Analysis of Evidence (AOE) Protocol, 33–35

analytical thinking, prompts for, 85

asset-based feedback, 26–27

asset-based learning, classroom practices for, 65

Baldwin, James, 135

belonging
    defined, 30
    invitations to create movement anchored in, 163–164
    prompts for, 85
    thinking benefitting from, 50, 51, 54

Bergman, Eyal, 137

bias, 109, 110–111, 149–150

Bloomberg, Paul J., 18, 114

brain development. *See* neuroscience

Brown, Ann, 20

Bruner, Jerome, 20

Buckheit, Joanne, 114

budgeting, participatory, 99, 145

capabilities, in 4 Cs, 138

CEL 5D+ Framework, 130

civic empowerment, 98, 100. *See also* democracy

civic reflection, 156, 158–159

Claim-Support-Question strategy, 86

classroom inquiry. *See* collaborative inquiry

classroom observations, 109

co-assessment, 92

cognition, in 4 Cs, 138

cognitive overload, 64

cognitive strategies, metacognitive strategies and, 44, 45

Collaborative for Academic, Social, and Emotional Learning (CASEL), 57–58

collaborative inquiry. *See also* Impact Teams
- classroom practices for, 65–66
- culture cultivation and, 103–108
- future of learning and, 154
- Youth Empowered Stewardship and, 120, 152

collective well-being (social awareness/relationship skills), example of, 58

communication systems, use of, 142

communities, as learning laboratories, 141, 142

community-building circles, 27

community engagement (responsible decision-making), example of, 58

community equity teams, 144–145

community walks, 141, 142

compliance, empowerment versus, 152–154

conceptual knowledge, defined, 42

Conditions for Success standard, 123, 125

conferences, student-led, 99, 147

confidence, in 4 Cs, 138

conflict resolution skills, interconnectedness of executive functioning, self-regulation, and SEL and, 61

Connect-Extend-Challenge strategy, 86

connections, in 4 Cs, 138

Costa, Art, 95–96, 100

critical self-reflection (self-awareness), example of, 58

cultural intersectionality, defined, 30

culturally responsive and sustaining practices
    example of, 67
    family-school partnerships and, 143, 145
    Impact Teams and, 127
    interconnectedness of executive functioning, self-regulation, and SEL, 59

culture cultivation. *See also* family-school partnerships; professional learning
    overview, 103
    collaborative inquiry and, 103–108
    family-school partnerships and, 147
    Metacognitive Equity Walks, 109–114
    reflection and action for, 120–121
    scaling of, 122
    student governance councils, 117–118
    student-led instructional rounds, 99, 114–117
    Youth Empowered Stewardship, 119–120

decision-making, democratic, 99

declarative knowledge, defined, 42

deficit beliefs, 53

democracy
    civic empowerment and, 98, 100
    culture cultivation and, 120
    metacognition and, 54
    metacognitive clarity and, 22
    principles in learning community, 22–23

professional learning for democratic agency, 130–132

prompts for, 85

purpose and, 69, 77

demonstrations of learning, flexibility in, 27

Dewey, John, 20

dialogue protocols, 87

Digital Citizenship Standards (ISTE), 157–158

digital platforms, collaboration and, 142–143, 144

disabilities, students with, metacognitive equity and, 18, 45

dorsolateral prefrontal cortex, 44

Dual Capacity-Building Framework, 125–126, 133, 137–138, 145

Dweck, Carol, 53

EAA (Evidence-Analysis-Action) Framework, 104–105, 126, 154

EAA (Evidence-Analysis-Action) Template, 113–114

Elgin Jr./Sr. High School, 129

emotional clarity, 35–36

emotional resilience, interconnectedness of executive functioning, self-regulation, and SEL and, 61

emotional safety, 35–36, 48, 50, 51, 54

empathy, commitment to, 163

Empathy Checks strategy, 97

empathy interviews, 141, 142

empowerment, compliance versus, 152–154

equity

AI and, 149–150

equity walks, 109–114, 154

ethics and, 156–159

Evidence-Analysis-Action Template and, 113

family-school partnerships and, 144–145

impact rubrics, 148

metacognitive equity, 17–18, 45, 48–54, 109

misinformation and, 158

prompts for, 85

for students with disabilities, 18, 45
equity walks, 109–114, 154
The Essential Conversation (Lawrence-Lightfoot), 133, 134–135
ethical guardrails for AI, 151, 156
evaluation. *See also* metacognitive cycle
    equity walks and, 111–112
    peer assessment and feedback, 92, 117
    questions for, 41
    student-led instructional rounds, 99, 114–117, 152
Evidence-Analysis-Action (EAA) Framework, 104–105, 126, 154
Evidence-Analysis-Action (EAA) Template, 113–114
evidence walks, 109–114
executive functioning, 20, 59–61
external rewards, 71

family advisory councils, 145, 146, 147
family conversation cards, 147
family learning workshops, 142, 144, 147
family-school partnerships
    overview, 133–134
    advancing metacognitive clarity with, 139–144
    collaborative inquiry and, 105
    collective agency and, 148
    as democratic practice, 144–145
    Dual Capacity-Building Framework and, 125–126, 133, 137–138, 145
    families as metacognitive experts, 138–139
    identity affirmation and, 49
    importance of, 17
    involvement versus engagement, 133
    learner identity and, 26
    overcoming barriers to, 145–148
    professional learning and, 125–126
    reflection and action for, 148
    tools for, 147–148

transformative SEL and, 57
trust and, 134–137
Finland, misinformation and, 157
fixed mindset, 53
Flavell, John, 15, 17, 20
flexible thinking, 95, 97
formative assessment process, 90–93
4 Cs, 138
funds of knowledge, 140
Future of Jobs Report (WEF), 151
future of learning
    overview, 149–151
    agency-driven approaches to, 151–152
    being part of metacognitive transformation, 159–160
    from compliance to empowerment, 152–154
    invitations to create movement anchored in, 163–164
    metacognitive clarity as ethical imperative, 156–159
    reflection and action for, 160–161
    self-directed learners and, 154–156

ghosts in the classroom concept, 133, 134–135
goal setting
    classroom practices for, 64–65
    co-construction with students, 74–75, 86–87
    example of, 67
    justice-centered learning goals, 70–74
    learner identity and, 27
    as learning-to-learn strategy, 80
    ownership clarity and, 92
governance councils, 117–118, 152
growth mindset, 53
growth portfolio systems, 144

Habits of Mind, 95–98, 100–101
Harris, Shadae, 140–141
Harvard Project Zero, 52n
Hattie, John, 17, 21
HCD (Human-Centered Design), 127
hippocampus, 50
historically marginalized students, metacognitive equity and, 18
history, present impacts of, 134–137
holistic learning
    overview, 56–57
    classroom practices for, 63–66
    interconnectedness of executive functioning, self-regulation, and SEL, 59–62
    metacognition and, 62–63
    neuroscience and, 63
home-school learning contracts, 143
Human-Centered Design (HCD), 127

identity
    affirmation of, 49, 51, 54
    invitations to create movement anchored in, 163–164
    learner identity, 25–31, 37
    personal identity, 25–26
    social identity, 25
identity, diversity, justice, and action (IDJA), Social Justice Standards and, 74
identity affirmation, 49, 51, 54
identity maps, 27
Impact Teams. *See also* culture cultivation
    overview, 33, 127–130
    Analysis of Evidence Protocol, 33–35
    benefits of, 35
    democratic values of, 131
    Evidence-Analysis-Action (EAA) Framework and, 104–105
    future of learning and, 154
    professional learning and, 124

implicit biases, 109, 110–111
impulsivity management, 96, 97
information literacy, 18, 84, 157–159
Inquiry Circles, 98
Instructional Leadership Teams (ILTs), 154
instructional rounds, 99, 114–117, 152
integrity, leading with, 164
intelligence, definition of, 53
interest-based projects, 26
International Society for Technology in Education (ISTE), 157–158

job skills, future, 149
journals, 66–67, 87, 148
justice-centered learning goals, 70–74

Kallick, Bena, 95–96, 100
Kamehameha Maui school, 128
knowledge types, 42–43

Lawrence-Lightfoot, Sara, 133, 134–135
leadership, student governance councils, 117–118, 152
learner agency, defined, 17. *See also* agency and autonomy
Learner Agency Tree, 27–29
learner identity, 25–31, 37
learning contracts, 143
learning disabilities, students with, metacognitive equity and, 45
learning dispositions, 35
Learning Forward Professional Learning standards, 123–125, 131
learning journals, 87
learning-to-learn, explicit teaching of, 78–81
learning walks, 144
listening sessions, 136–137

listening with understanding and empathy, 95, 97

local data, analysis of, 141, 142

making thinking visible, 51–52, 86–87

Mapp, Karen, 133, 137

McGuire, Saundra Yancy, 109, 156

media literacy, 18, 84, 157–159

medial prefrontal cortex, 26

metacognition
- defined, 15
- democracy and, 54
- families as experts in, 138–139
- as Habit of Mind, 95, 97–98
- knowledge types and, 42–43
- learner identity and, 31
- social-emotional learning and, 62–63
- teaching craft of, 51–52
- timeline of, 19–22

metacognitive clarity. *See also* culture cultivation; future of learning; goal setting; ownership clarity; process clarity; purpose clarity
- overview, 36
- benefits of, 15, 17
- democracy and, 22
- emotional clarity and, 36
- as ethical imperative, 156–159
- importance of, 22
- invitations to create movement anchored in, 163–164
- learner identity and, 25–31
- progressions for, 88–89
- prompts for, 84–86
- scaling of, 129–130, 159–160, 162
- shifting from teacher clarity to, 17–18, 32–33
- transformative power of, 46–47

metacognitive cycle

overview, 16, 38–41, 78–79
benefits of, 43–44
learning-to-learn strategies and, 79–81
metacognitive strategies and, 45–46
modeling of, 15
naming and sharpening, 19
reflection and action for, 24
weaving into learning experiences, 81–84
metacognitive equity, 17–18, 45, 48–54, 109
Metacognitive Equity Walks, 109–114, 154
metacognitive strategies, cognitive strategies and, 44, 45
Michael J. Petrides School, 129
midway monitoring check-ins, 82
mindfulness, 66–67
misinformation, 18, 84, 157–159
monitoring, 41, 110–111, 116. *See also* metacognitive cycle
Muhammad, Gholdy, 25
multilingual learners, metacognitive equity and, 18

neurodiverse learners, metacognitive equity and, 45
neuroscience
- co-construction with students and, 99
- collaboration across generations, 119
- emotional safety and, 35–36, 50
- executive functioning and, 59
- holistic learning and, 63
- imagination of future, 159
- learner identity and, 26, 49
- metacognition timeline and, 21
- misinformation and, 157
- purpose and, 71
- reflection and, 44, 84, 104, 157
- routines and, 64
- self-regulation and, 21, 59, 95

observations of classrooms, 109
ownership clarity
    overview, 90
    civic empowerment and, 98, 100
    democracy and, 99–100
    Evidence-Analysis-Action Template and, 113
    formative assessment process and, 90–93
    Habits of Mind and, 95–98, 100–101
    reflection and action for, 100–101
    success criteria, co-construction with students, 86–87, 93–95

Parent Advisory Committees (PACs), 146
parent-student-teacher conferences, 99, 143, 147
participatory budgeting, 99, 145
Pause-Reflect-Act strategy, 97
peer assessment, 92
peer feedback, 117
persistence, 95, 97
personal identity, 25–26
Plan–Monitor–Evaluate cycle. *See* metacognitive cycle
planning
    equity walks, 110
    as learning-to-learn strategy, 80
    prompts for, 81–82
    questions for, 40
    student-led instructional rounds, 116
pockets of excellence, 122
post-task evaluations, 83–84
prefrontal cortex, 44, 50, 59
procedural knowledge, defined, 42
process clarity. *See also* metacognitive cycle
    Evidence-Analysis-Action Template and, 113
    importance of, 87–88
    learning-to-learn, explicit teaching of, 78–81

making thinking visible, 86–87

prompts for, 84–86

reflection and action for, 89

professional learning

democratic agency cultivation and, 130–132

families as co-learners and, 125–126

Impact Teams and, 127–130

reflection and action for, 132

scaling with, 122–123

Project Zero, 52n

PS 9 Naples Street Elementary, 128

PS 16, 129

psychological safety, 35–36, 48, 50, 51, 54

purpose clarity

anchoring learning in community, contribution, and criticality, 76–77

benefits of, 69

co-construction with students, 74–75

democracy and, 69, 77

Evidence-Analysis-Action Template and, 113

justice-centered learning goals and, 70–74

puzzles of practice versus problems of practice, 104, 106–108

questioning as Habit of Mind, 95, 98

reflective thinking and practices

civic reflection, 156, 158–159

classroom practices for, 63–64

on educator biases, 109

equity walks and, 111–112

family-school partnerships and, 146–147

future of learning and, 163

Habits of Mind and, 98

invitations to create movement anchored in, 164

John Dewey and, 20
journaling and, 66–67
as learning-to-learn strategy, 81
neuroscience and, 44, 84, 104, 157
ownership clarity and, 90–91
structures for, 99
Youth Empowered Stewardship and, 120
relationships, interconnectedness of executive functioning, self-regulation, and SEL and, 62
resilience, 44, 61, 144, 146
responsible decision-making (community engagement), 58
restorative circles, 99
restorative justice practices, 99
rewards, 71
rigor, democracy and, 22
Rigorous Content for Each Learner standard, 123, 124
routines, 64

safety, 35–36, 48, 50, 51, 54
Sanford B. Dole Middle School, 129
See-Think-Wonder strategy, 86
SEL competencies (CASEL), 35
self-assessment, 27
self-awareness (critical self-reflection), 58
self-efficacy, 30, 62
self-monitoring, as learning-to-learn strategy, 80
self-regulation. *See also* holistic learning
  defined, 61
  family-school partnerships and, 146
  metacognition and, 59
  metacognitive cycle and, 44
  neuroscience and, 21, 59, 95
  SEL and, 61–62
Simmons, Dena, 57
Skills Imperative 2035, 149

social awareness/relationship skills (collective well-being), 58

social-emotional learning (SEL), 61. *See also* holistic learning

social identity, 25

Social Justice Standards, 74

speech recognition systems, 150

standards, 74, 123–125, 131, 157–158

Stop-Think-Reflect strategy, 97–98

student governance councils, 117–118, 152

Student-Led Civic Hackathon Protocol, 156

student-led conferences, 99, 147

student-led instructional rounds, 99, 114–117, 152

Student-Led Rounds (Buckheit & Bloomberg), 114

success criteria, co-construction with students, 86–87, 93–95

systemwide alignment, 130

take-home metacognitive toolkits, 143, 144

Tatum, Beverly Daniels, 25

teacher clarity, 17–18, 25, 32–33

thinking. *See* reflective thinking and practices
- analytical thinking prompts, 85
- belonging benefitting, 50, 51, 54
- flexibility in, 95, 97
- making visible, 51–52, 86–87

thinking routines, 51–52, 86

30-60-90 day plan to scale metacognitive clarity, 159–160

Transformational Processes standard, 123, 124–125

Transformative Social-Emotional Learning (tSEL), 56–58

trust, families and, 134–137

Try 3 Before Me strategy, 97

Universal Design for Learning (UDL), 56

Visible Thinking routines, 51–52

The White Man's Guilt (Baldwin), 135
workshops, family learning, 142, 144, 147
World Economic Forum (WEF), 149, 151
Wormeli, Rick, 53

youth advisory councils, 99
Youth Empowered Stewardship (YES), 119–120, 152
Youth Participatory Action Research (YPAR), 99–100

Join Our Impact Team Community

Join our learner-centered PLC community where we put students in the driver's seat!

Let's create schools that work for all of us!

Build multigenerational partnerships with **YES! (Youth Empowered Stewardship).**

Competency Over Conformity

Embrace the power of personalized learning and unlock your potential with Competency-Based Learning.

Literacy and Justice for All

Discover the power of a comprehensive, research-based literacy education that meets the needs of every student.

Thank you!

Mimi & Todd Press exclusively publishes authors who are dedicated to making an impact through their work. By purchasing, reading and implementing their ideas, you deepen the impact and increase awareness for future learning.

More from Mimi & Todd Press:

Leading Impact Teams: Building a Culture of Efficacy and Agency
Paul Bloomberg and Barb Pitchford

Re-Envisioning Rigor Books 1, 2 and 3
Michael McDowell and Aaron Eisberg

Belonging Through a Culture of Dignity: The Keys to Successful Equity Implementation
Floyd Cobb and John Krownapple

The Project Habit: Making Rigorous PBL Doable
Michael McDowell and Kelley S. Miller

Amplify Learner Voice through Culturally Responsive and Sustaining Assessment
Paul Bloomberg, Kara Vandas, Ingrid Twyman, et al.

Peer Power: Unite, Learn and Prosper: Activate an Assessment Revolution
Paul Bloomberg, Barb Pitchford, Kara Vandas, et al.

Arrows: A Systems-Based Approach to School Leadership
Carrie Rosebrock and Sarah Henry

Learner Agency: A Field Guide for Taking Flight
Kara Vandas, Jeanette Westfall, and Ashley Duvall

mimitoddpress.com

Mimi & Todd Press discovers and publishes purpose-driven thought leaders who are striving to make a difference in the world. Visit us online to browse our catalogue of books and learn more.

www.ingramcontent.com/pod-product-compliance
Lightning Source LLC
Chambersburg PA
CBHW040000080526
44586CB00027B/2826